McENROE

McENROE

The Man with the Rage to Win

Tania Cross

ARROW BOOKS

Arrow Books Limited
17–21 Conway Street, London W1P 6JD

An imprint of the Hutchinson Publishing Group

London Melbourne Sydney Auckland
Johannesburg and agencies throughout
the world

First published 1982

Set in Linotron Sabon
by Rowland Phototypesetting Limited
Bury St Edmunds, Suffolk

Made and printed in Great Britain
by The Anchor Press Ltd
Tiptree, Essex

ISBN 0 09 928780 3

Contents

I would like to dedicate this book to my parents, Brian and Audrey Cross, for their continual support, and to Graham for his understanding

Acknowledgements

My gratitude is directed to the following people, for without their help the book would not have been completed:

Dick Gould for his time and co-operation while I was at Stanford; Barry MacKay at the TransAmerican Open in California; John Newcombe and Dennis McElrath for their hospitality in Fiji and Sydney; Alan Little for kindly compiling the statistics; John McEnroe's friends and fellow players; José Neves; Linda-Marie Singer; Murry Janoff; the press, worldwide; the magazines *Tennis USA*, *World Tennis*, *Tennis Australia*, and *Tennis World*; and finally to Jane Judd, my persevering editor.

List of Illustrations

Sometimes the only parts of a city a touring player will see are the airport and tennis courts.

John, like many pros, spends much of his time on the tour in his hotel room.

John and Stacy get together after the WCT finals in 1981.

John takes his duties seriously when at press conferences.

Madame Tussauds immortalize the 1981 Wimbledon champion.

Full concentration is needed for every point.

John vents anger at officials by breaking his racket, and clowning.

John cools himself off, and readjusts and checks strings which are continually breaking.

Reigning champion Borg poses with McEnroe at the start of the final in 1981.

John becomes the new champion after a gruelling five sets.

John the rock star joins Barry Beck of the Rangers at a benefit.

The McEnroes enjoy the discotheque.

A victory dinner for the Davis Cup team, McEnroe, Connors, Ashe and trainer Bill Norris.

John meets Borg again in the US Open and again is the victor.

A controversy rages round John at the Benson & Hedges tournament as the champion rests on a linesman's box.

The Early Days

John Paul McEnroe was posted to Germany in the late 1950s by the American air force with his young wife, Kay. On 16 February 1959, whilst living on the military base at Wiesbaden, just outside Frankfurt, their first son was born. John Patrick McEnroe started his life of travelling at the tender age of nine months, when his parents flew back to the United States, their home country.

A graduate of the Catholic University in Washington, twenty-five-year-old McEnroe was determined to become a lawyer so he worked in advertising to support his family, while studying law by night at Fordham University. It was tough in those days because he did not get home until around ten o'clock and then he had to study for his classes the next day and still make it to work in the morning.

On 2 February 1962 their second son, Mark, was born, and on 1 July 1966 Patrick completed the family.

At their comfortable home in Douglaston, which is a suburb of New York, Kay brought up her three sons. She was registered as a nurse, but the three boys kept her days fully occupied.

John started his elementary education at Buckley

Country Day School where he attained very good grades, and then he moved on to Trinity, a preparatory high school. 'He was a competitor in the classroom,' said his mother. 'Whatever the best mark was, he wanted it too. He worked hard. At 7.20 a.m. he would take the train to Manhattan. School started at 8.20 a.m. and let out at 4.10 p.m. then he'd play sport and get home about 7.15, have some dinner and study. So it was a long day for him.'

Although John was brought up in a well-run middle-class home, some say that it was Trinity School that made him into the tough, street-fighter kid – that combined with his Irish Catholic ancestry. Growing up in New York is hard; it is one of the most formidable, competitive cities in the world.

From an early age, John was a keen sportsman, and played soccer at Trinity, and although he may not remember it he first hit a ball with a plastic bat at the tender age of eighteen months.

Strangely enough, John remembers very little about his childhood. 'My parents never really spoke to me about their life in Germany, so I don't feel any particular connection there.' When John reached the age of twenty-one he had the choice – by law – to request a German citizenship. He thought they might ask him to represent Germany in the Davis Cup, but no one contacted him.

'I have a bad memory,' he said. 'I'm not one of these people who can remember things that happened to them when they were three years old.' He says he really cannot remember anything before the age of ten. 'I'm not joking,' he laughed. 'My only bad memory from my childhood was when I ran into a tree on my bicycle. That was the worst experience of my life. It happened on Thursday the twelfth, and even to this day if the twelfth lands on a Thursday, I don't go out.

'Oh, and I guess I remember my brother being born when I was seven.'

However, he has no trouble recounting the scores of his matches when he was eleven: if not the actual points, then certainly the game score.

The McEnroe home is only two blocks from the Douglaston Club on Little Neck Bay, a quiet community suburb of New York. When John was ten, the family joined the club for its social values, not for sports. But soon John and his father, followed by the two boys, discovered the tennis courts.

John's first racket was one which had been discarded by a family friend, Frank Prior. The first one bought for him was a discount store model that he used in the clinics given during his first couple of years at the club.

John's talents were so promising that Dan Dwyer and George Seewagen Sr, the pros giving the clinics, soon recommended that the McEnroes develop them. So little John went to an old Mexican Davis Cup player, Antonio Palafox, who happened to be working at Port Washington during that time, and asked for lessons. Tony then became the head pro at the Cove Racquet Club in Glen Cove on Long Island, just a short drive from the McEnroe home, and so John went with him and remained under his tutorship for six years. Harry Hopman, who mainly looked after Vitas Gerulaitis, helped with the coaching and later took over.

John surprised everyone by reaching the semi-finals of a twelve-and-under tournament. He lost, but only a month later he had his first tournament win.

'When John went to his first nationals he was only eleven,' his mother said. 'We still laugh at this. He had only one racket and we worried what would happen if he lost the racket. I drove John and his father to the airport and we stopped at the club on the way. We went on court and took Mark's racket out of his hands to give to John as a second racket. Poor Mark, he thought he was being punished.'

'Funny, today John goes off with a dozen rackets under his arm and nobody thinks anything about it,' his father said. 'I remember at a tournament some years ago over-hearing a couple of kids talking. One said, "There's John McEnroe, he's a good player." The other kid said, "How can he be a good player when he only has two rackets?"'

Palafox declared that it was his concentration which put him above the other kids of his age. 'Like a lot of kids today,' said his coach, 'he has to learn to control emotional outbursts, but a lot of people don't understand that these are a result of his concentration. He'd get angry at himself when things didn't go right. Other kids had more talent but couldn't do the things John could do at his age because nobody could really concentrate like he did.'

Fellow juniors noticed that on occasions young McEnroe came off court almost in tears if he had lost a match. If anything was going to tame his temper it would have been suspension in those early days when he desperately wanted to win and to prove himself. That is the age when it hurts the most – Bjorn Borg knows this only too well: when the Swedish Tennis Federation banned him from tennis and his mother locked his racket in a cupboard, and look what it did for him.

The Mexican was asked to train the McEnroe's youngest son as well. 'They say Patrick was better at eleven than John was at the same age,' said McEnroe Sr. 'But at eleven, John had only been playing for three years, whereas Patrick had played for eight.'

The similarity between John and Patrick is evident in their appearance. The younger has the same penetrating, intelligent eyes of his brother, but inherited the straight brown hair like Mark's. Patrick is said to be a polite fifteen-year-old showing a lot of promise in his ability to hit a tennis ball. Although he is still studying at Trinity, 1981 saw him compete in the Orange Bowl world junior championships, which is for players from twelve to eighteen, a title won by John in 1976. Patrick defeated Peter Moore of Great Britain in the first round 6–4 6–3, playing on the public courts at Flamingo Park, but lost to Fernando Boese of Brazil in the second 7–6 7–5 6–1.

The youngest McEnroe draws as much interest as does the baby of the Evert family, fourteen-year-old Clare, and it can put pressure on them. 'I don't feel that I have to live up to John's reputation, although many people seem to think I do,' Patrick said. 'I never will be as good as John, who has unbelievable talent.'

Mark also plays tennis, but never earned a number one ranking in the Juniors. He still plays occasionally in tournaments like the Irish Open – the home of their ancestors, but he has no intention of joining the circuit full time.

'Mark is the last player in the team,' grinned Patrick. 'He'd rather go to the beach or hang out with the girls, but he is very smart.'

After prep school in Connecticut he enjoyed his first year at Stanford, studying political science, and he is thinking of following his father's footsteps by going to law school. Although Mark has made it to Wimbledon for the past couple of years, he doesn't see much of his elder brother these days but says, 'We have become more like friends than brothers in the last two years.'

Palafox said at the age of twelve it is impossible to tell if a kid has got what it takes to become a champion, but at the age of seventeen he was certain with John. 'I felt then that he could do absolutely anything,' he said.

Once John had swept away all the twelve and under titles, he won the Orange Bowl and then he and Larry

Gottfried won the Sunshine Cup. Gottfried had beaten him to the No. 1 position in the sixteens in 1975 and the eighteens in 1976.

In 1977, he went on to play a couple of Bill Riordan's tournaments in Ocean City and Virginia Beach, and lost to Ilie Nastase in each, going out in the first round, at Ocean City, but in the second tournament he beat Charlie Pasarell and Bob Lutz and then extended Nastase to three sets. 'That is when he started thinking he might have something,' said his father. 'He went to Dallas to play in the WCT Juniors and then went to Europe for the first time.'

His exploits in Europe have been recounted many times as he reached the top on the Potential List. He won the French Junior title, qualified for the French Open and won a match, but lost to Phil Dent in five sets. However, in the mixed doubles, McEnroe was lifted to the heights by Mary Carillo, a twenty-year-old Douglaston neighbour. It was the first time they had played together in a tournament and they won the title, beating Florenza Mihai and Ivan Molina. They both leapt high in ecstasy before shaking hands with each other and then their opponents. Mary went on to a career in broadcasting and John went on aimlessly without her, failing to win anything in Paris since.

Then John qualified for Wimbledon, where he bowed out of the Juniors to concentrate on the men's singles. He reached the semis, beating Phil Dent in five sets this time.

'It was as big a surprise to us as it must have been to John,' his father said. 'We hadn't planned to go to Wimbledon. But when he got to the semis to play Connors, Palafox and I went over there.'

John had already accepted the scholarship from Stanford, long before Wimbledon, and so he had to turn down about $50,000 in prize money to remain eligible.

The year of 1978 was to be a year of decisions for John McEnroe. Offers for endorsements and guarantees came flooding in from all over the world. His apparent possible worth was incredible. His parents were torn between wanting a good education for their son, and the realization that he would probably be tempted to the million-dollar circuit. 'We want the best for our son,' they agreed.

Kay McEnroe reflected that it takes a lot of discipline to turn down the kind of money that is waved at youngsters these days. But they kept telling John that he could only be an eighteen-year-old freshman in college once, and his father had hoped that he would get some business education because he didn't want to see his son teaching backhands at forty.

By that time, McEnroe Sr had established himself as a Park Avenue attorney. He was, and still is, a partner in one of the nation's most prestigious law firms, Paul, Weiss, Rifkind, Wharton & Garrison, where he specializes in corporate and securities law. With these qualifications he was capable of estimating what success as a tennis professional could mean for John.

'His mother and I were pleased that he decided to stay an amateur and enter Stanford, because we believe in education, but I honestly didn't think he would stay long. I'd be kidding if I said I thought he would have finished four years of college as an amateur,' said John Sr.

If John had waited until he graduated, he would have been twenty-two, which is almost too late to start a career in pro tennis, although a few players have done it, Roscoe Tanner and Stan Smith, for example.

John's father tried to look at the situation with a more practical eye, and suggested that his son be a part-time pro. Working on the theory that if John Jr could earn $50,000 from his first summer of major competition and not even win a tournament while doing it, he could undoubtedly win a lot more as he got older and more experienced. So he could perhaps have played on the circuit in the summer and attended college in the winter.

'But I realized the argument against this idea,' said his father realistically. 'You don't do justice to either . . . being a pro tennis player or being a student.'

John agreed to try university, so he went off to Stanford in California. His mother smiled. 'The house was sort of quiet with both John and Mark at school. John's room is very neat these days.'

Stanford University

Leland Stanford, governor of California in the mid-1800s, became a very rich man through the success of the railroads and also acquired vast amounts of land as payment. On this land he decided to raise and breed trotting horses. Sadly, the Stanfords' only child died suddenly at the age of sixteen of typhoid fever, whilst travelling with his parents in Europe. Stanford University, which is still nicknamed 'the Farm', was built as a memorial to Leland Junior in 1891. His father said at the time: 'Any place that is good enough for raising race horses ought to be good for students.'

The university basks in 8000 acres of rolling hills, golden fields, wooded retreats, streams and lakes. In fact, the campus is so large that the students get around on bicycles. This can become quite precarious as they wend their way to lectures through the sandstone arches on wet, slippery mornings, balancing an armful of books. And it does get wet in California. John said with distaste: 'There was a lot of rain. It would rain thirty-five days in a row and the temperature change was amazing. In the morning it would be 80°F, by three o'clock it would be 85°F and then at night the temperature dropped to 40°F. I used to get a lot of colds.'

The central feature of the college is known as the 'quadrangle' – or 'quad' in student language – which is a huge courtyard with open-arched corridors, giving it a Spanish flavour. A beautiful church faces into the quad, decorated with bright mural paintings. Many of the original buildings were damaged in the 1906 San Francisco earthquake and so the reconstruction, which is still taking place today, must meet California's safety standards, as tremors are quite frequently felt.

Probably one of the most well-known landmarks is the Hoover Tower, built by President Hoover in the 1900s as a rebellion against Marxism. It houses three million books on war, revolution and peace.

The college breeds success and is free to those who have the excellence to get in with a scholarship. For the rest, tuition costs $10,000 a year. Stanford not only has a good reputation in sport, but is also recognized as having some of the finest medical, business and law schools in the States, and the list of student achievements is never-ending. In sport, it boasts the best facilities, coaching and competitive opportunities. And with that formula, some of the world's top sports personalities have been born: Jim Plunkett of American football, Tom Watson in golf and, of course, John McEnroe.

Not all the credit can be given to Stanford for producing John, as he was already a brilliant player in his own right; after all, it was in 1977 that he had blasted his way through to reach the semi-finals at Wimbledon.

With his obvious talent, it made people wonder why he disregarded the advice of Guillermo Vilas, among others, and elected to attend school. But when McEnroe was offered one of Stanford's five full scholarships in 1978, he saw it as an opportunity to get the grounding he so desperately wanted, before embarking on a career which was to take him on to the gruelling circuit of professional tennis. 'I just wanted the experience of being like everybody else for a year, that's one reason. I wasn't ready emotionally to play professionally as I had never spent much time on the circuit, and I think a lot of these young kids don't realize how tough it is to travel around and they think they can just walk out and play really great.' He explained, 'It is tough when you are alone in Australia or South America, where you don't feel comfortable. So I just wanted time to prepare myself mentally.'

He continued, 'It was already decided. I mean I was one of the top juniors then and as long as you're smart enough to get into the school, you can pretty much pick and choose where you want to go. All the kids in America have to take the SATs – Scholastic Aptitude Tests – and it also depends on how you did in high school. If you fail every course, you are not going to get into Stanford, but I was a B student, and I had an above average report, and being good at tennis helps,' he grinned. John was good enough at soccer that the Stanford coach asked if he'd be interested in playing soccer at college as well as tennis.

'I wasn't definitely sure till about January '78 that I was going to turn pro,' John stated. 'It was important for me to win the NCAA title and, in any case, I wasn't what you'd call a great student. Basically, I just took the general courses that all freshmen take, introductory, economics, psychology, maths. Oh, I was good at maths,' he laughed, then added, modestly, 'but nothing extraordinary.' Those, however, were not the sentiments of his maths professor who said that he had excelled in the subject, with his quick mind and thinking capabilities.

John was a conscientious worker, even if he does deny being academic, and that in itself is a sign of a perfectionist. He is always striving to do everything to the best of his ability. 'I do a pretty good job of upsetting people wherever I go,' he said with irony. During the spring semester in which tennis was played, he would take night classes once or twice a week, so that he could finish his lectures at about twelve or one o'clock and then play tennis for the rest of the afternoon.

While studying at Stanford, John remained on the campus. 'I lived in one of the dorms, the Riconda dorm. I was just like the other students,' he stressed firmly. 'My room-mate was a track and field guy; he threw the discus and things like that. He was a big guy,' said John, expanding his chest to demonstrate, 'so we didn't have too many arguments. There was a guys' floor and a girls' floor. Now they have a mixed floor.' He pondered on this with amusement for a minute and then continued. 'The social life was quite good but obviously it was a little different for me because, you see, I was known by then, and it was kind of tough when I first got there as I came to school a week late. I had been playing in the San Francisco tournament and didn't come up to Stanford until after everyone had registered, so they had already got to know a few people. But it was okay after a while; there were parties and I hung around with Peter Rennart, who was in the second year, and a lot of his friends. Played basketball and stuff. That's how I hurt my ankle, you know. I sprained it three times playing in college.' John still has to wear bandages occasionally to support his ankle when he is playing. He is really keen on soccer as well, specifying that American football is too dangerous.

The comments from those days in the *Stanford Daily*, the campus rag, make interesting reading as they were just beginning to realize the calibre of a player within the folds of their campus.

On 7 April 1978, the paper quoted Dick Gould, the coach at Stanford for the past sixteen years, as saying: '"McEnroe is definitely my best player."' It continued, 'John McEnroe, Bill Maze, Perry Wright, Matt Mitchell,

John Rast, Peter Rennart and Jim Hodges produced the best collegiate team in two decades,' even though John had a knee injury that year which kept him out of some of the collegiate matches.

April 20th brought more news: 'McEnroe, currently ranked 15th in the world, faced freshman Eliot Teltscher. Ilie Nastase calls Teltscher the "best young player in the United States". Teltscher's only loss in 14 matches came to McEnroe in Los Angeles 2–6 7–5 6–3,' they reported with obvious pride.

The summer of '77 had been a dream vacation for McEnroe. After warming up with wins over big-name pros Charlie Pasarell and Bob Lutz, the talented 18-year-old decided the fooling around was over. He smashed, spun and argued his way through Europe to the semi-finals of Wimbledon where it took Jimmy Connors five sets to beat him. According to Mac it's all "pretty much probable" he'll turn pro after the Cards defend their NCAA crown 22–29 in Georgia. Dick Gould was obviously delighted when McEnroe chose to spend a year on 'the farm'. But the situation could have been very disruptive to team unity. If Mac was a cocky petulant brat as the papers had characterized him during the summer, his presence would have hurt rather than helped the Cardinals. But that problem did not exist according to Gould: 'John was one of the most outstanding players I've ever had. He would bust his tail for anyone on the team. He's the first guy down on the court to console a teammate who lost and the first guy to congratulate a teammate who won. He projects an interest in other people.

After losing to McEnroe, the paper quoted Matt Mitchell as saying, ' "The best way to beat him was to hire an assassin! He can hurt you with so many things. He has incredible control. He hits hard and accurate and the way he plays is very unorthodox." McEnroe is unorthodox, but you cannot argue with success. He doesn't bend his knees much, often doesn't step into the ball, and uses an incredible amount of wrist on nearly every shot. If beginners start imitating him, tennis elbow could be the next world-wide epidemic,' the paper finished.

John was to become the subject of more journalists' stories, and the topic of more conversations than probably any other sportsman in the world.

Before what John refers to as 'the Wimbledon thing', meaning his success in 1977, he had thought about graduating, but ended up finishing only one year at Stanford. 'I wish that he could have had a normal college career,' said his mother, Kay. 'But in my heart I knew he was too talented to wait.' She laughed when she remembered the time that she had to settle down and accept that she may have raised a professional athlete and John added, 'I didn't regret leaving college, but then I didn't regret going there.'

Three years later the story takes us back to California. It's a warm, sunny day in September, and Dick Gould is sitting on the sofa in his small 'homely' office. The walls are covered with photographs of tennis champions, those who have made it on to the pro circuit and those who played purely for the love of the game. Gould is a tall, good-looking man in his early forties, with a slim, healthy build and warm eyes which crease at the corners when he smiles. He is good at handling people and is one of the few fortunates who know the other side of McEnroe. Relaxed, he leans against a cushion and contemplates the man the public know – the shouting, arguing McEnroe. 'I think as a coach that this cannot be doing him any good. Then I realize he is a rare person who thrives on this combative experience,' he explained. 'John's personality profile would make a special study, for he is a living contradiction at times.' Dick moved forward to impress his next words. 'He has a tremendous quality to him which I only wish people could get to know. Of course, he doesn't have a heart of gold, but John was the one his teammates respected and admired. Full of good fun with a little psyching spirit thrown in. If our last man needed a point to win a crucial match, John led the rooting.'

Outside, strains of music fill the air from a string quartet. People are laughing and chatting as they hold their glasses under the silver wine fountain and dip huge, juicy strawberries into bowls of cream. The scene is reminiscent of an English garden party, or perhaps of Wimbledon many years ago.

Gould is responsible for whipping up this little piece of magic. As he proudly presents the show for the day, all the ex-Stanford players who made it into the world's top forty, join him on the tennis court and line up in front of the net! Roscoe Tanner, Pat Dupre, Tim Mayotte, Gene Mayer and John McEnroe. One of America's latest young prodigies, nineteen-year-old Scot Davis, is there along with Nick Saviano, Jim Delaney and Peter Rennart, although injury prevented Peter taking part. The occasion was to raise money for the Stanford Tennis Professional Endowed Scholarship. These men have flown from different parts of the world to be together on this Sunday afternoon, charging no expenses. As far as McEnroe is concerned, Dick is a friend who gave him a great deal of help, and returning the favour in any way he can is a priority because loyalty to his friends is paramount.

He had been playing a series of exhibition matches against Vitas Gerulaitis. On Tuesday they were in Denver, Thursday in Seattle, Friday in San Antonio, and in Houston on Saturday where John was still on court at midnight. He got about four hours' sleep and then flew down to San Francisco, arriving an hour and a half before he was due to play. He drove to Stanford in a hired car and forty minutes later he was on court playing Gene Mayer – admittedly looking somewhat jaded. 'I was beat,' he confided. 'I think it was just getting there, being around a little, that was important.'

Tim Mayotte had an exhibition match in the morning for the Peugot–Rossignol team against Johan Kriek. The heat was suffocating as they made it through two sets. Then, forfeiting the after-match cocktail party, Tim rushed straight off court, jumped into a car and drove for half an hour up to Stanford.

Nobody can say that these players put nothing back into the game from which they reap such rich rewards.

McEnroe, even if he was playing through half-closed eyelids, still managed to entertain the crowd. The relaxed ambience of the audience – probably enhanced by the white wine – created a feeling of warmth and security. Here the players were away from the pressures of winning, from the agents, the press, the officials and the hostile crowds. John responded to this, as did the others.

Early in his match with Mayer, a double fault was called against Mac. He grinned, looked twice at the linesman and everyone laughed. Mayer hit a good serve and John yelled 'You're supposed to be taking it easy on me,' to which Mayer replied, 'You've gotta realize we are all exhibitionists here!' The game continued in this mood, much to everyone's delight.

Looking exasperated as a ball whizzes past him, John does a Nastase act and gives the linesman his racket and promptly sits down. On the next point, John serves an ace, the crowd leap up, cheering, and he raises his arms in triumph. Mayer drives a ball hard to the baseline which Mac runs for and cries, 'Oh, shit!' as he tries a flick return with his back to the court. It doesn't work. The crowd go wild, caught up in the fun of the occasion. The players are on a platform to entertain and the people love it. The crowd are restless in anticipation, the tension rises as Gene races into the lead. At break point Mac pleads in mock anguish, worthy of a Shakespearian actor: 'Put me out of my misery.' Smiling benignly, Mayer hits a winning forehand down the line to lead 5–2.

The next rally is pure gold. Beautifully angled shots are played as if the word pressure does not exist. Mayer effects an incredible shot between his legs to win the point. John just collapses on the court in amazement. The little heap picks himself up and returns to the baseline, getting ready to receive service with his back to the court.

Even in this utopia one of the line judges gives a few dubious calls against Mac. Gene shouts over, 'Don't worry about it, he was my roommate.' Mayer then cracks a great serve, so John points to the linesman on his side and says, 'He was *my* roommate and that was out!'

The shrieks of laughter bring students rushing over to the courts. They clamber up into the trees to watch, peer through holes in the fences and crawl under the hedges: eager young faces in brightly coloured sweat shirts.

All the players put on a show of equal calibre, so as the sun goes down and the day draws to a close, people drift out, happy and probably feeling a little honoured that they had seen the controversial figure of John McEnroe actually enjoy the game he plays so well. He lost – maybe there is a moral in that somewhere!

Those four hours raised over $40,000 for the scholarship system.

Superbrat or Superchampion?

The man nobody understands hurries to the lifts in the hotel lobby, past the reporters trying to catch a word, past the flashing white lights of the photographers, through the autograph hunters thrusting pen and paper in front of him.

The man is tired and seeks refuge in the quiet of his hotel room. Just another week, another hotel, and another country.

His tousled brown hair is as unruly as the man himself, and at the age of twenty-two, anxious furrows show on his brow from the pressure of the life he leads. The intense green eyes view the intruders of his peace with suspicion as he makes his way.

When John McEnroe came over to play at Wimbledon at the age of eighteen, he hit fame with amazing rapidity, because of his success as a qualifier and unfortunately for his volatile behaviour on court. He stood out in the gentlemanly game of tennis because he was different, a rebel, and suddenly he was in demand. People on the streets recognized him, press from all over the world wanted to speak to him and the television companies requested his presence.

Exposure to such a degree can be daunting, particularly for a nervous, highly strung person such as he. Being of a shy nature his awkwardness with strangers was mistaken as rude insolence which gave him the 'superbrat' image.

He was greatly misunderstood in those days and, once branded with an unfavourable reputation, it is hard to correct. The English saw him as a spoilt, bad-tempered American kid who needed a good clip round the ear and some manners drummed into him. His lack of respect for his elders caused hackles to rise.

A newcomer in any situation has to ease his way into acceptance, but McEnroe bulldozed right in, making it quite clear what he wanted and had no qualms about expressing his views on people. Another element which is very strong in his character is that of perfection. John gives his utmost, and he always plays to the best of his ability. He cannot abide slackness or incompetence from those around him and is quick to criticize, which has not made him popular. He is incensed by an audience who does not understand or appreciate the art form which he is attempting to perfect. 'You know nothing about tennis,' he shouts with venom at the offenders. They just laugh and continue to bait him, eager for the moment when he will crack.

The majority of spectators who are subjected to McEnroe's tirades deserve it, but sometimes he makes mistakes. One time two fans became terribly upset when, having attended the Benson & Hedges tournament at Wembley every day to watch his matches, even wearing 'McEnroe the greatest' T-shirts, he suddenly turned on them and started shouting abuse, thinking it was they who had been jeering at him. Absolutely distraught, they wrote a letter to him in the hope that they could explain the situation.

This is where superstars have to be careful, whether they are in films or sport, as any word they say to an ordinary individual will be remembered for life. Quite

31

simply, if it is a kind word they will love him, if it's harsh they will hate him.

Bill Scanlon, a player from Texas, was once asked why he didn't yell at the ball boys, like McEnroe has been known to do. He replied, 'I was a ball boy once. What is the point of shouting at them? They are doing their best. It's like asking for autographs. When I was awestruck by these guys, I mean they were superstars . . . something special. If I asked for their autograph and they shouted at me, it would make me feel really horrible. I'd feel bad for a couple of days,' he said shaking his head at the memory.

McEnroe does not really hate the crowd around him as much as it sounds. He was asked if he would prefer to play without an audience. 'Oh no,' he replied with a straight face. 'Who would you have to get upset about?' Then he smiled. 'That's part of the thrill. If you were number one and nobody gave a damn, I am sure you would wish that people did. I like people to leave me alone but if I was number fifty I would probably want them to come up and bug me or whatever. So you want your cake and to eat it too. Of course you want the people.'

John even admitted that when he was a kid he used to ask for autographs. Rod Laver was his idol when he was growing up. 'I like signing for the young kids, but not the ones who have bet their friends a buck that they can get your autograph. They don't care about it and throw it away.'

Through bitter experience, John has come to realize how tough it is to play when the crowd is against you and the press are writing damning articles about you every day.

Over the last year he has improved considerably in the public eye. Always in the past when attending press conferences, he would fidget, pluck nervously at his hair and could never look the questioner directly in the eyes. He used to drop his gaze and shift uncomfortably under the scrutiny of the world's press. His mumbled sentences stopped in mid-flow and then started again on a different line as he tried to put across his point.

Now his answers are coherent and concise, and he will discuss relevant topics with interest and credible knowledge. He appears to have relaxed to a certain extent into the position of the number one player in the world, and is accepting the added responsibility which he feels goes with the title, like commitments to tournaments and sorting out politics in tennis. 'He has changed,' said his long-time girlfriend, Stacy Margolin. 'Why, at the age of sixteen when we first met, he hardly said "please" or "thank you" to anyone. Now he's appreciative, he's softening, all right. He just needs some refining here and there . . .'

John is modest of his talent as a player, making the excuse that tennis came easily to him and so he has never really had to work at it. His modesty even extends into his home, where he asks for all the trophies that have been won over the years to be kept from general view. 'He doesn't have any of them in his room,' said his mother. 'We've taken some of the major ones and displayed them in the dining room and living room.'

'I've been fortunate,' he claimed. 'I'm good at something which is rewarding financially and mentally. I mean I never dreamed I could earn this kind of money. It's ridiculous, really. I hit a ball with a racket.'

Put into that kind of perspective, the game does seem a little crazy: people walloping a felt-covered ball back and forth, watched excitedly by thousands of avid eyes. But it is none the less a game which commands great skill. A few simple mistakes on a player's part can make the difference between success and failure. A close contest generates tension among the crowd and the tension converts into pressure on the players. John feels this intensely, especially as he has progressed further in the game. 'When people come to see me in a tournament, they are not coming to see me play, they're coming to watch me win. If I don't win, I feel bad, like I let everybody down. God!' he said with agony, 'I hate that feeling.'

It is because John is sensitive to his responsibilities that he has built up a good reputation with teammates, sponsors and tournament directors. 'I've never seen him go back on a commitment,' said his close friend, Peter Fleming. 'I mean, here is a guy who has played Davis Cup competition every year that he's been asked, at some considerable financial sacrifice,' Peter concluded.

The Davis Cup has always been important to John. During the spring term of his final year at Trinity, he used to travel with the Junior Davis Cup squad, and then in 1978 he played his first match on the senior squad against Chile in Santiago and has represented his country ever since.

'It was something that was in my head when I was younger,' he admitted. 'My parents wanted me to play as well. I think the competition lost some of its attraction to the public at one time, but it is starting to get it back now. At least in Portland [Oregon] when we played Australia, the crowds were really good. I like taking part in team tennis because you can openly root for guys. On the tour you can't do that as it will cause bad feeling. But on the team you get to know the guys really well and I always have a good time.' Then he added thoughtfully, 'It's like doubles to some extent. You help each other, which is something you don't get to do very often.'

In October 1981 Roscoe Tanner was the second singles

player for the semi-finals tie against Australia. He had a tough five-set match against Peter McNamara which he eventually won with a few tips from John McEnroe. Davis Cup is unique in that there is a ten-minute break after the third set when the coach or members of the team can talk, and discuss tactics with the player.

'After I lost the third set,' said Tanner, 'John came up and was telling me about different things I could do to maybe win the fourth set.' Then he added, 'John was very much part of the team the whole week. He is a team sort of player, doing whatever is required to get himself playing better, as well as all the other guys. I think that speaks very highly for him, being the number one player. A lot of number ones don't really try to help anyone else. He helped all the time in practise to get the guys playing the way they wanted which a lot of the guys in the US don't do.'

The semi-final tie was played in good spirit, supported by a crowd of 12,000 packed into the Memorial Coliseum in Portland.

With the two singles matches under their belts (McEnroe beat Mark Edmonson), the Fleming/McEnroe team faced Peter McNamara and Phil Dent for the doubles.

The Americans clinched the first two sets 8–6 6–4 and it was at 2–2 deuce with Dent serving in the third set when the trouble broke out. Richard Evans, who was at the scene of the crime, reported: 'Fleming played a ball which landed on the line and the linesman called it out. McEnroe didn't bother to move for the McNamara volley, but when the linesman covered his eyes signalling unsighted, the umpire acted on the fact that the ball had been good and so announced advantage Australia. Correctly, McEnroe and Fleming complained they had been distracted by the call, but the umpire would not consult his linesman, even though the official admitted to Fleming that he had indeed called in the middle of the point. McEnroe started complaining to Ashe who spoke to the umpire and got no response. Fleming then started yelling at the Canadian referee, who said he had no power to instruct the umpire as to what he should do under the circumstances. The argument raged for five minutes and eventually Fleming flung down his racket in fury and earned the United States their second conduct warning. (A brief outburst in an earlier game from McEnroe, gave them the first warning.) Play was resumed and the Americans won 6–4 in the third.'

The previously patriotic atmosphere changed to one of uncomfortable embarrassment.

Arthur Ashe said, 'The umpire was wrong, but I was disgusted with the way my players reacted and I told them so.'

McEnroe's comment was: 'I know we were in the right, but we screwed up again – don't tell me, I know we screwed up.'

The 1981 Davis Cup final against Argentina witnessed another dramatic doubles match. At the Riverfront Stadium in Cincinnati McEnroe and Fleming took 4 hours and 52 minutes to defeat Guillermo Vilas and José Luis Clerc 6–3 4–6 6–4 4–6 11–9. A verbal battle of insults between the players flared up during the match, causing the Danish referee, Kurt Nielsen, to ask the two captains, Arthur Ashe and Carlos Junquet, to sort their teams out.

The fifth set lasted for 89 unbearably tense minutes, as each game went with serve until Fleming lost his in the thirteenth. But McEnroe was not to be beaten. With two great passing shots, a killing smash and a fault from Clerc, Vilas's serve was broken.

McEnroe won his serve and the team took Clerc's, giving America a 2–1 lead over Argentina.

John had a long and tiring five-set match against Clerc, beating him 7–5 5–7 6–3 3–6 6–3 and the United States celebrated their 27th victory of the Davis Cup.

Vilas and Tanner played the final dead rubber, but after twenty-one games in front of a near empty stadium, both teams agreed to call it off.

Throughout the tie, McEnroe and Ashe appeared to have arguments over John's behaviour.

The superstar said afterwards, 'It's really tough being captain. The players expect him to do something and the press expect him to do something else. [The press] are quick to criticize the players rather than Arthur because he has a well-deserved reputation. But I am trying to win and Arthur is trying to win, although we have different ways of doing it. It is obvious that I am a lot more emotional, but if we were just everyday people I'm sure we would get along fine. In these situations it's a little tougher, but when you win the cup a lot is forgotten.'

A former Wimbledon champion, Arthur Ashe is the first to acknowledge how much depends on McEnroe to pull the United States through and has been trying to encourage Jimmy Connors to join the team to alleviate some of the pressure from John. Connors played only one of the four ties in 1981.

McEnroe's behaviour has come under considerable criticism during the past two ties, and rightly so. However, during a match against Ivan Lendl, when America played Czechoslovakia, he behaved impeccably, somewhat to the disgust of some black spectators who said, 'You keep bein nice, McEnroe, and you ain't gonna win!' So who do you please?

John is not as ruthless as the majority of people make out, and his basic values are very commendable. But he is an intelligent guy and knows a touch of adverse psychology does not go amiss on his opponent.

Whilst he has his friends on the circuit, he also has a few enemies. Silent feuds take place on court unbeknown to the spectators, except they may perhaps witness a ball being blatantly drilled at the rival's body. The unpleasantness is rarely taken off court: it is purely his intense competitiveness that feeds it, although one player was amused to find that, whilst he and McEnroe had always been on good speaking terms, John refused to acknowledge him after losing to him in a match.

His strong presence may intimidate a few officials, but most of them admit he is usually correct on about 75 per cent of the calls he questions, and his opponents state that his interruptions in the game do not put them off. As Connors said, 'I'm out there fighting for my rights too.' John feels that you should not be a top player if it does affect you. 'I'm not saying that I think it's something that should be done all the time, though,' he added.

John has been accused in the past of being a bad sport because he doesn't acknowledge a good shot from his opponent. 'For me it would be phoney,' he reasons, 'to clap on my racket or say good shot, because I always feel that I should have hit a better shot the one before. Sometimes a guy will play a great stroke and I think people appreciate that, but a lot of them don't know the reason he can hit it so well is because you have hit a lousy approach shot and that is why I get upset at myself. I don't consider that bad sportsmanship. I consider it trying to win.'

At times McEnroe goes slightly overboard with his arguments: in fact, he seems to manage it every time he steps on court. Hopefully, age and experience will quieten this characteristic, as it has done with some of his elders. Dennis Ralston was once suspended for bad behaviour, and now he is one of the most respected men in the game.

Some people do not seem to mind his behaviour. One spectator commented after Wimbledon, 'In my opinion his play is so good that one can almost forget his indiscretions,' whilst another growled, 'McEnroe is nothing but a cheeky, spoilt, bad-tempered pup . . .'

It is noticeable that when John reaches the final of a tournament he rarely behaves badly, with exception, of course, to the Wembley final in 1981 against Connors. 'Once you get to the finals, it's like you're *there*,' he explained. 'I feel the pressure more in the early rounds because you are always expected to win. Everybody asks me why I don't get upset when I'm playing Borg. Well, when I eventually reach Borg, it's what everyone has been waiting for, but most of them want him to win, so the pressure is lifted slightly from me, and losing to Borg in the final is not exactly like losing to Joe Blow in the first round – it is not altogether a lost cause.'

Borg is one of the few people who exact McEnroe's full concentration. He doesn't have time to dispute calls, because all his strength is directed towards Bjorn.

Problems arise when Mac faces a lesser-ranked player in the early rounds. The player is good, but John knows he can beat him. If he takes an early lead he starts becoming distracted by things around him. He notices every little movement in the crowd. He wanders around the court, scuffing the floor and patting his short curly hair. With one hand in his pocket, he swings his racket around loosely. 'Sometimes I find myself getting lazy on court. I'm just content to play from the baseline instead of moving into the net,' he admits.

It is when he finds himself in this frame of mind that he gets angry; he needs to fire himself up to concentrate, otherwise 'Joe' will blow him off the courts.

It is interesting to learn how Mac tries to beat an opponent. After his semi-final match against Eliot Teltscher in Sydney, John talked to the press.

'I thought Eliot was great,' he said. 'He definitely made me work for it. Those are the guys it is satisfying to win against, because they make you work hard. I think you have to mix the game up with him. He likes pace so I tried every type of shot. These balls are heavy, so it is tough to come in on your second serve, but especially against him because he goes for winners. So I figured I'd just stay back and work for it. I wasn't going to move in unless I had a really good shot. Sometimes I get in the habit of just chipping and coming in on pretty much anything, but that is what he likes, so I only came in to the net when I was seventy-five per cent sure I was going to win the point.'

McEnroe wins by analysing the opponent's game, by utilizing his weapons to prize open their weaknesses. Most of the 500 ranked players can hit a backhand and forehand, but they cannot play the big points like McEnroe, and that is the factor which makes him a champion.

John Newcombe rates Mac as a better player than Laver was at his age. Rod's great strength was in his ability to change tactics halfway through a game, and this is just what John is capable of. He does not play with the 'hit it as hard as I can' game of Connors, nor the patient, waiting game of Borg. He will lure and manoeuvre his opponent with chips and dinks, and tempting short balls, until the prey takes the bait, then whacks the ball straight down the side line with a flick of the wrist.

Arthur Ashe captured the essence of his talent when McEnroe was still in his teens. 'Against Connors and Borg you feel like you're being hit with a sledgehammer, but this guy McEnroe has a stiletto; he just slices you up.

He has a ton of shots – a slice here, a nick there, a cut over there. Pretty soon you've got blood all over you. The wounds aren't deep, but you bleed to death.'

Laver took up Newcombe's verbal challenge and replied, 'In my day we were a little more suited to grass than the players of today. But on slow indoor surfaces or clay, they would have the advantage. Ground strokes are better than ten or fifteen years ago, which makes these guys a little stronger on slow surfaces. We played mostly on grass courts and the faster moving ball suited us better, particularly when it came to the serve and volley game.' The forty-three-year-old tennis millionaire admitted that he would love the chance to take on McEnroe when he was at his peak. 'I like playing the best. That is why I became a professional in 1963.' The 'Rocket' believes that Junior takes the title as 'Best Player in the World' but Borg has not had his last say. 'I think anywhere but on clay McEnroe can probably beat Borg. There isn't any real weakness in John's game. He has a lot of natural talent but doesn't have the experience or the confidence to beat Borg on clay.'

The twenty-two-year-old agreed with the words from the 'wise one'. 'I don't think I'm really ready to play on clay yet.' This slow, taxing form of tennis is not suited to Mac's 'quick death' game. He would have to train hard to be any good on this surface: building up his fitness and stamina for those forty-five to fifty stroke rallies, and learning to concentrate for long periods and to be patient, cool-headed.

The clay-court players are really the only ones who could pose a threat to his number one supremacy. 'Borg is not quite out of the picture yet,' he states solemnly. 'He is only twenty-five. And Lendl is younger than me, he's twenty-one. Clerc is a year older. But I think Ivan Lendl is probably the top shot for number one, although I don't think he has developed the all-round game yet. He is tough on clay, and it would be really hard for me to beat him on that surface right now, as I proved at the French Open. Borg, Lendl and Clerc are the guys I wouldn't want to face.'

The computer system can confuse the issue of surfaces, as John pointed out. 'I didn't play Clerc once in a Grand Prix tournament for the whole year, nor Vilas or Gene Mayer, and I only played Connors right at the end of the year. So you can be in the top ten, say between five and ten, and only be good on one surface. That's a bad system.'

It is frustrating to observe the totally relaxed, almost disinterested manner in which McEnroe attains such high standards as he strives for perfection. However, he does not feel he is even close to that level. 'It's pretty tough to get there, and probably I never will,' he said with honesty. 'But I really feel I can improve: you know, I played some pretty bad matches this year.' The essence of improvement in John's eyes would be to cut down on the bad matches and thus become a more consistent player, and he feels the need to get stronger physically and mentally, so that he is comfortable with every aspect of his game, all the time.

The excitement and chaos generated by Wimbledon or the US Open keeps the adrenalin pumping in everybody's veins. Demands are made on the players from every side. TV and radio interviewers want them, there are press conferences to attend, agents and sponsors to see, and fans follow them around all the time. On court the pressure weighs heavily, but it keeps the player keyed up and sometimes forces the best tennis out of him. So when McEnroe wins that final point of the final, the release must be immense. Two days later he is expected to play in a small $175,000 tournament and to build himself up again to produce the same quality tennis in the first round as he had to win the championships the previous week.

'You have just got to give it the best you can under the circumstances,' was his theory. 'But I prefer to be beaten because the other guy beat me. Not for other reasons.'

On the physical side of Mac's game, he believes he can improve even further, which must be a worrying prospect for the majority of players. 'I think my ground-strokes have improved in the last six months, although they are still not as good as I would like them to be. I get lazy on my volley and serve,' he admits. John's serve is one of the strangest parts of his game. He stands with his back almost to the service court, then leans down low with his weight on the front foot to bounce the ball, then rocks back and forward and serves. This rocking motion developed because of a problem with his back. There is actually a missing link in his spine and this movement helps to release the tension.

Strength is another aspect he seeks to improve his game. 'I need to get stronger in the upper body so that I can maybe muscle a few balls, hit the ball harder when I need to.'

John really dislikes having to practise and never trains during a break even if its as long as three weeks, so it is hard for him to stay fit. 'Last year,' he said with disdain, 'I was about a hundred and eighty-two pounds and was eating around fifteen meals a day. It became a major problem just to get out of bed. Now I've cut down on junk food and beer and I'm a hundred and fifty-seven or eight pounds so it's a lot easier to get out on court. That's why I intend to keep at that weight, just for that reason. But,' he laughed, 'King's Cross in Sydney is a haven for junk food.'

McEnroe is not fond of running and is even reluctant to do stretching exercises before a match, and therefore is prone to injury. In the past he has played with strapping on his upper leg to protect a pulled thigh muscle and with bandages on a twisted ankle. There are always bruises, blisters and other little aches and pains to deal with and this is the job of the ATP trainers. Bill Norris and Dave Fechtman travel on the circuit to look after the physical well-being of the players. McEnroe usually gets one of them to give him a rub down before he goes on court.

Peter Bodo, an American journalist, reported how, 'after taking a nasty tumble in the Masters, McEnroe recalled an incident which transpired during a junior tournament in Kalamazoo.' John refuses to be beaten by the ball and so will go to any length to run it down. On this occasion, he bore down on one particular ball with such intense determination he ran head on into a light pole and knocked himself out. 'They gave me twenty minutes to come to,' he laughed with little apprehension for his welfare.

The young American's main goal is to stay number one for a while and to win the major events. He does not put much importance on breaking records, though.

'You're the people who look that stuff up,' he retorted when the press raised the subject. 'I would never have known that Bill Tilden won the US Open three years in a row if people hadn't told me, and I just happened to read somewhere that I was the only person in thirty or forty years to have won the singles and doubles in the US Open and at Wimbledon, but I would never have known that, so all those things are nice, it's like gravy.'

'You are not trying to carve your niche then?' he was asked.

'I think that is the wrong way to look at it; there is more than enough pressure now, so I don't try to add to it. I have had more than my share of problems and pressure for a lifetime. Saying that I have to win Wimbledon five more times is not going to help me.'

It seems that John's greatest desire is to be respected for his game, although few players would argue that he deserves to carry the title of number one in the world. 'Oh, I think I am respected for my play,' he said. 'But I think the other part might overshadow it right now. That is Nasty's problem. I mean, it has been his trouble all through his career. People are going to remember the way he acted.'

This factor obviously bothers Junior to quite an extent, and until he can break out of the vicious circle which ensnares him, he will continue to maintain this reputation. For as long as he conducts his on-court tantrums, the spectators who fill the seats will be sensationalists, looking for a fight, hoping to aggravate him until he explodes, and whilst they buy the tickets, the people who really have the knowledge to appreciate tennis will stay at home. 'I guess I've always had a temper,' he said with a shrug. 'But I'm trying to change.'

McEnroe has been classed as a genius by some and an eccentric by others. Whichever category covers him, his game is truly amazing. The wide left-handed serve causes even the greatest of his opponents serious problems. He can play every shot in the book and many which have not been written about yet. His top spin backhand and forehand is produced with infuriating ease, and his speed around the court intrudes on the privacy of every square inch.

For a man who really does love the game, it is puzzling to see him always looking so miserable. 'I don't like to smile,' he said with a heavy frown. 'This is a serious business, you know.' Then he brightened a little. 'I don't get depressed, I just get irritated with myself, that's all.' He followed on to say that he was not the type of person who would, for example, leave a place because he was feeling down. 'Everyone gets moments of homesickness, but I have never caught a plane home because I was depressed. I always find something to do if I have lost.'

Over the years many of the players have developed superstitions when they play, which they now find hard to discard. Bjorn Borg is well known for his beard growth at Wimbledon: in fact, his superstitions developed into a yearly ritual at this tournament. He would stay at the same hotel, practise at the same club, travel the same route to Wimbledon, have the same locker and even place his towel on the same spot after each changeover. Interestingly, he stayed at a different hotel for the 1981 championships. Perhaps that had something to do with his loss.

Vitas Gerulaitis will never walk on the lines if he can help it, and Nastase says that if he is winning a tournament, he will wash his shorts and socks in the sink every night so that he can wear them the next day.

'I have my superstitions,' said Mac, 'but they vary from week to week, and if I lose they all go out the window.'

Free Time and Friends

For a man who is a household name, John does not consider himself a celebrity. 'I don't like what goes with it. I don't like being phoney and that's what happens when you start meeting hundreds of different people all over the place. I think being honest is more important than being liked by everyone.'

John McEnroe Sr describes his son as a quiet and shy individual, but thinks he has a terrific sense of humour. Unless you are one of his close friends, however, you are unlikely to witness his true form. Off court John keeps very much to himself and shares his company only with a few close and trusted friends.

Peter Fleming is a good-looking blond from New Jersey. At 6 feet 5 inches, he looks as though he should have been a basketball player. However, he proved his ability at tennis by winning a scholarship to Michigan and then another which took him to UCLA where he won the All-American title and was runner-up for the NCAA title in 1976.

These days Peter and John are the best doubles team in the business and also are the best of friends. These two have had a few laughs over the four years they have been together, and they have won as many as thirty-four doubles titles in the process.

Peter is often the peacemaker on court, intervening between John and the umpire or linesman whenever possible. He insists that it is John's expressions which get him into trouble. His pale, pugnacious face scowls and pouts at noisy spectators.

As a singles player, Fleming has never really enjoyed the success his talent deserved. 'Peter doesn't move too well in singles,' explained his partner. 'But we complement each other in doubles because he is big and I can move around at the net.'

In January 1982 Peter, partnering fellow American Fritz Buehning while McEnroe competed in another tournament, struggled to get a foothold in the Barratt World Doubles in Birmingham. The pair won only one set out of their first three matches. Rather than being the demoralizing experience it seems, Fleming felt that he gained immensely from the competitive play. But he did feel that his own game had faltered over the past eighteen months and wanted to improve for the sake of his partnership with McEnroe.

'In our first year together, we were able to play really competitive practice sets against each other and it improved our games. It would be good for both of us if I could improve and push John again in practice.'

To be at the top in both games must be admired, because different strategies and tactics are involved for each and even different shots are required. John enjoys playing singles and doubles, it also keeps him match sharp. Although he does state quite adamantly, 'I don't play doubles unless I like the person I'm playing with. Peter is my best friend on the circuit and I like Ferdi [Taygan]. I just won't play at all unless I like them, but,' he said with a grin, 'I can usually find one person I like in a tournament.'

Fleming's views on his partner are favourable as well. 'I

can't think of anyone better to play with than John,' he said. 'He appears to get upset with referees and linesmen, but he has never got mad with me, and I can tell you there have been times when I deserved it. He says that we work as a team and that's all there is to it. I hate a crowd to be against me. Life is too short to have to go through that kind of aggravation. John and I are both upset with a crowd when they egg us on and so it helps to have someone there going through the same thing.'

Of course it is inevitable that they meet in singles competitions. During the year of 1979, two weeks after they had won the US Open together, they reached the men's singles final of the Jack Kramer Open in Los Angeles. Peter won 6–4 6–4 and said after collecting his winner's cheque, 'I know he won't want to hear this but I would like to thank John McEnroe, for without his support I wouldn't be playing the way I am today.' From Los Angeles they went to San Francisco and faced each other again in the final. This time McEnroe won 4–6 7–5 6–2. 'I dread playing Peter more than anyone else on the circuit, including Borg and Connors,' he reflected later.

Like McEnroe, Peter has a reputation for being honest and frank, and his humour can be disarming at times, as he proved on one occasion in 1979. He and John had just managed to take the title of the Braniff Airways Doubles after a difficult final against Sherwood Stewart and Ilie Nastase. With two volatile characters on court, there were a few fireworks, but nothing too serious.

After the match, the winners were requested to attend another presentation and to give speeches. This customary reception was attended by many of the tennis socialites and important people. As they laughed politely and sipped their champagne, McEnroe and Fleming ambled in. John was terribly nervous as he thanked the tournament director and the sponsors; he found it hard to look up into the sea of faces and shifted uncomfortably, so Peter took over the show. He chatted with ease and when asked about the match, he quipped with superb timing, 'Oh, we were lucky to win, especially having an asshole like him for a partner!'

Sadly, Peter had a bad year throughout 1980; he lost a lot of first-round matches, but the most damaging was his loss of confidence. He even tried one of the large Prince rackets, but that did not solve his problem. In this frame of mind, John found it difficult to have confidence in his partner's play. Peter said at the time despondently, 'Whereas a couple of years ago we would just blow guys off the court, now we are struggling.'

The year of 1981 was an improvement, and the desperately needed confidence was restored tenderly. They won the doubles championships at Wimbledon beating Bob Lutz and Stan Smith, and the US Open against Gunthardt/McNamara and retained their status as number one in the world. Even so, Peter could be excused for a slight distraction: he announced his engagement to Jenny Hudson, an English model, that year. They plan to marry on 17 July 1982 at the Methodist church in Wetherby, a little country town in Yorkshire. The couple had originally decided on a date in May, but the crowded tournament schedule would have made it difficult for their tennis friends to attend. As best man, John will have to look after Peter for a change, and speeches will be made in a marquee as the reception is to be held in the garden. He will surely have some amusing tales of bachelor life on the circuit.

Jenny and Peter have bought a house in London, so perhaps this twenty-seven-year-old will not be around to keep his partner in check quite so much in the future.

Fleming, who is a very easy-going sort of person, has helped to bring out some of the quick wit in McEnroe.

Together they manufacture one-liners like they were going out of fashion. Unfortunately the treatment he receives in England never allows him to relax and joke around with the crowd. His matches, however, are not always totally devoid of humour. Whilst playing in Sydney, John spotted a little boy in the front row eating an ice-cream – admittedly the child's mother was a shapely blonde – and Junior went up to the youngster and said something to the effect of 'That ice-cream sure looks tasty.' The boy gleefully handed over his revolting-looking pink and purple 'Mr Blob' and John took a bite.

Another amusing incident occurred, again in Australia. It is a well known fact that John gets a little irritated when people move around the stands during play, so when one man marched on to the court in the middle of a doubles match, McEnroe, quite understandably, couldn't believe his eyes. 'What the hell do you think you are doing?' he asked incredulously, whilst Fleming looked on. The guy threw a fervent glance in McEnroe's direction and hurried determinedly to the umpire's chair to the utter amazement of all four players. The umpire then announced, 'If there is a doctor in the stadium could he please go to the front entrance.' There was absolute silence for about ten seconds and then one doctor got up, then another and another until there were doctors rushing from every section of the arena much to the crowd's amusement. A few points later, when play was resumed, John hit a forehand deep to the baseline which was called out by the linesman and several people behind him. McEnroe shook his head and allowed a grin to creep slowly on to his face. 'Gees, you've got seventy doctors and five hundred linesmen!' he quipped.

In spite of all the interruptions, the number one duo managed to win that match, which took them into the finals the next day.

McEnroe had to play his singles first and won, beating Roscoe Tanner. He was allowed half an hour's rest before going on court for the doubles, so, as the pressmen all had their deadlines to meet, he consented to give an interview during this break. It was interesting to see how easily John conversed with the Australian press; in fact, everyone became so relaxed enjoying the chat that the time ticked away unnoticed. Suddenly there was an almighty bellow in the corridor. '*Junioooorr . . . !*' Then Fleming put his head round the door and said with a sheepish grin, 'C'mon, we have got a business to attend to out there.'

Unfortunately, to the embarrassment of some, McEnroe's one-liners are not always humorous and he has in the past found himself involved in a heated argument with a member of the audience, usually as a result of that person applauding a double fault or deliberately baiting him.

Bud Collins, the American NBC broadcaster, said John nearly ended up with a broken nose from one combat, when the lady's husband stood up and said, 'Say that again, sonny.' As Junior abhors violence and this guy just happened to be around 240 lbs, he shut his mouth and turned back to the game.

Fame is a strange phenomenon. For some, being famous allows you to have the ordinary people running around after your every whim and at the same time lack of privacy is enough to drive the average person around the bend.

John McEnroe Sr remarked on how unaffected his son was by his success. 'Friends tell me how unchanged he is,' said his father. 'Fame has absolutely not gone to his head.' Whether it affects him or not does not alter the fact that he is a renowned person, and it is not an easy position to cope with, especially with his shy, nervous nature. Somebody once commented on his nervousness and said, 'If McEnroe was a concert pianist he would be throwing up in the wings before every performance.'

His ability to play tennis to such a high standard has brought him into contact with many more people than the average twenty-two-year-old would expect to meet. Some of them are well known and others are business associates, but they all have to be dealt with in the correct manner, and that is not a skill which comes naturally. John decided that honesty at all times was the best solution. 'They might not appreciate hearing my opinions, but I think being honest is more important than being liked by everyone.'

Recognition, of course, has its advantages. It gave him a ringside seat at the star-studded Tommy Hearns v Sugar Ray Leonard fight which took place at Caesar's Palace in Las Vegas last September. John is really not keen on violence in any form, so whilst Elizabeth Taylor jumped up and down with glee as the punches were thrown, Mac remained slightly pale and unmoved as he sat next to his basketball friend, Larry Holmes. After the fight, a cock-tail party was given for the guests and the superstar of tennis felt very insignificant as he mixed with some of the Hollywood greats.

McEnroe is not totally alien to the film world. A few years ago a movie called 'Players' was made, featuring Dean Martin's son, Dino, and Ali McGraw. The story was about a tennis 'bum' who made his money as a hustler. A friend of his would entice some poor old man to bet on a match between Martin and his opponent, the outcome of which was always fixed. The player rose from the depths of tennis hustling to the heights of Wimbledon, and along the journey he falls in love with a rich lady.

Quite a number of pros took part to give the film a touch of authenticity. Pancho Gonzales played Martin's coach, and Guillermo Vilas took the part of his opponent for the Wimbledon final, which really was filmed at the all England Club.

McEnroe makes his appearance fairly early in the film. He is practising with Gonzales when Martin walks in and challenges the old coach to a game to prove that he is as good if not better than his latest protégé. So John lends him a racket and steps aside to sit on the sidelines to watch. Can you imagine John really doing that? The filming for that sequence took place in Las Vegas. 'I only had three lines in the movie,' said John, laughing, 'but I was there for two days. Can you believe it took two days to film my three lines? The waiting on a motion picture set is incredible. I liked it a lot, though. Who knows, I may even go into it permanently when I retire from tennis.'

If he does not make it as a film star the rock scene will certainly attract him.

John has always been a music fan and never travels without his tape deck and a Sony Walkman wrapped around his neck for company. His love for music was evident after he heard of the tragic death of John Lennon. McEnroe insisted on one minute's silence for the fomer Beatle before the start of the WCT Challenge Cup final in Montreal. The tribute coincided with the world-wide memorial for Lennon at 2 p.m. in Central Park. One of Lennon's most popular songs, 'Imagine', was played in the auditorium while the WCT TV people put together a Lennon montage for live broadcast.

When arriving in a city for a match, the players always look out for concerts or good football matches. Having to play matches when there is a good group in town can be somewhat frustrating. One of McEnroe's favourite rock artists, 'The Boss' Bruce Springsteen, was performing in Memphis at the same time as John was playing a tournament there. As Mac was keen to attend, he went to the referee, Roy Dance, to request an earlier starting time for his doubles match with Peter Fleming. Unfortunately, they could not make any changes in the schedule and so John played his match and finally got there halfway through the three-hour concert. He managed to see the group again after his Wimbledon triumph.

Once, at a concert in New York given by reggae star Peter Tosh, McEnroe was spotted in the crowd and pulled up on to the stage, and one summer he and Peter Fleming actually performed on stage with Eddie Money in Central Park. His latest appearance was after the United States beat Czechoslovakia in the Davis Cup. Arthur Ashe, the captain, organized a celebration dinner for the team, but McEnroe was late because he was 'jamming' with Carlos Santana at West Side Pier in New York. Junior came on stage wearing a sleeveless T-shirt and dark shades. With his new short hair cut he certainly looked the part and proved that his talents extended past swinging a tennis racket around as he stood shaking a tambourine in one hand and a beer bottle in the other. Santana later appeared on NBC TV and said he had been delighted to have the new Wimbledon champion joining him on stage.

Since then Mac has bought himself a guitar, but he cannot play proficiently yet. He is, however, determined to become a rock star, much to the amazement of those in the tennis world. 'I'm serious,' he said. 'I would like to be a rock and roll star.' As the lifespan of a tennis player is relatively short, John said he likes the idea of being in this scene for a couple of years. Admittedly, his temperament would probably suit the role of a rock star much more comfortably than it does as a tennis star.

Fame shows its advantages again to the privileged few when, while the world's lesser mortals queue for hours in the cold for a meal at Park Lane's Hard Rock Café, they can get a table straight away. John frequently goes to the Hard Rock, which is an American-style hamburger joint, and is the subject of one of Carole King's songs. The loud rock music drowns conversation and the walls are hidden by posters and flags. They even managed to get old rackets from Mac and Jimmy Connors to put on the wall.

Another restaurant John makes a point of visiting when he is in London is Alexander's in the King's Road. He became friends with proprietor, José Neves, and his wife, Amanda, before he was really known in England. 'Even then,' said Amanda, 'he was shy. On one occasion he came in to give José a couple of tickets for Wimbledon. "He's not here at the moment," I told him, "but come in and have a drink." He wouldn't, though. He just hovered around the door and then waited in the next room.'

One year the couple threw a party and invited a whole crowd of Wimbledon players. A beautiful cold buffet was laid out on the tables and conversation bubbled like the champagne. John arrived with Stacy, wearing his usual brown jacket and blue jeans, but was so disappointed when he found his favourite pasta dish was unavailable that José had to light the ovens and cook a special meal for him. As it was a warm evening, he sat outside with Stacy at a table on the pavement to avoid the crowded restaurant.

At this party, José presented him with a cartoon caricature which a friend of his had drawn. Junior loved it, but when McEnroe Sr saw the drawing, he cried out in mock horror that John was not wearing Nike shoes in the picture, so it was taken back and altered!

The owner of Alexander's was very chuffed because McEnroe had hit a few balls with him at Queens Club when he was in London for the Benson & Hedges tournament in 1981. When José went down to the locker room at Wembley stadium to say good-bye to his friend who had just lost the singles and doubles titles, he was astounded when the first thing John said was, 'Now I want to see an improvement in your backhand by the time I return to England.'

It is when being famous becomes a disadvantage that one needs friends, and José has assisted John on several occasions.

After his triumph at Wimbledon, the press hounded him from every corner. On the day he was due to fly out of London, José received a telephone call from the British Airways girl who organizes the players' flights. In a panic she told him that terminal three was crawling with photographers. Jumping into the car, he drove at high speed to John's flat in Chelsea and relayed the story. They planned to hide the champion in the Concorde lounge until all the passengers had boarded and then whisk him through ·without the photographers knowing. In theory the idea seemed sound, but in practice it did not work.

Heathrow is divided into two sections in the terminals: airside and landside. To reach airside one needs a pass. A number of photographers managed to obtain these, and so when McEnroe appeared they rushed forward to try and get in front of him. In their haste, cups and saucers went flying and passengers were pushed impatiently aside as McEnroe was hustled through to the plane by the British Airways staff.

Apart from restaurants, every city has its regular night spots which the players adopt for one or two weeks of the year. In London Pontevechios and Stringfellows are favourites, and they get preferential treatment. Vitas Gerulaitis can saunter in wearing denim which is usually forbidden. But then no one minds what Vitas wears as long as he is there.

The blond man from Brooklyn New York is supposed to be the playboy of the circuit. 'We are all given labels,' said McEnroe. 'Borg is known as the quiet one, Connors is the tough one, Vilas is the poet and me . . . I'm called "Superbrat".'

As for the disco scene John says, 'I tend to avoid the "in" places because I don't much like them; sure, I've been to the occasional trendy disco, but that's really not my scene. To be honest I'm a lousy dancer.' But he admitted shyly that if he was asked to dance and the music was the right beat, he would probably have a go.

In Monte Carlo he showed he was capable of letting off some steam, whatever beat the music was. The last time Mac played at the country club there was for the 1980 championships. This event has been nicknamed the wives' tournament as all the players bring their better halves. Monaco is a glamorous, expensive stop on the tour and the pros are out for a good time. Most of them only play the tournament to make up for what they are going to lose at roulette tables in the famous casino or through their spouse's fingers. The avenues, boutiques and restaurants are full of beautiful rich people who create an atmosphere which invites everybody to taste their world.

During the championships, WCT held a Brazilian night for all the players, press and others involved in tennis. Elegance spun its way through the guests. Notorieties such as Princess Caroline, Phillippe Junot, Stirling Moss and Jackie Stewart were present.

After an impressive meal the evening swung into action as everyone moved over to Jimmy'z disco. Guillermo Vilas, Carlos Kirmayr and Tito Vasquez (Victor Pecci's coach) were in their element, singing South American love songs at the tops of their voices, whilst José Luis Clerc tried to do the limbo and crazy Nastase wound human chains through the dancing bodies. All those invited had dressed up for the occasion, even McEnroe and Gerulaitis wore suits and ties, but Ilie turned up in a bright sloganed T-shirt topped with a bow tie.

The music grew louder, the rhythm pounded and the people went wild. On-court rivalries melted in the heat and laughter as Bjorn, Mariana, Vitas, John, Ilie and Regine danced together, fighting for space on the crowded floor. The night finally slowed down into morning and people drifted happily away, all but Nastase, who lingered until 5 a.m.!

The principality of Monaco is such an attractive place to live that two of the players, namely Bjorn Borg and Guillermo Vilas, have bought apartments there. Monaco is also kind on them tax wise.

John has not invested any money here yet. He already has a flat in Manhattan and has recently bought a condominium at Turnberry Isle in Florida near Vitas Gerulaitis. He celebrated the acquiring of this new asset by inviting a few friends over. Early in the evening he went to the bathroom and then found he couldn't get out. It took security guards and maintenance men about an hour to get the door open. John then went into the bedroom and got locked in again! The locks had not been fitted properly and all the doors had to be replaced.

Apparently John now wants to install a Space Invaders machine, for the odd few hours when he has got nothing to do!

During those rare weeks when John takes a break from tennis, he spends as much time as possible with a lady who knows him very well, the pretty Californian girl, Stacy Margolin.

They met at sixteen while playing in a tournament in the Catskill mountains, a resort area north of Manhattan, and they played in the college teams at the same time, although Stacy was attending the University of Southern California, while John was at Stanford. The couple started dating seriously when they were eighteen.

Having someone to share the success, the failures and the frustrations of life is important, especially in the world of professional sport.

Stacy is petite, only 5 feet 3½ inches, and has a well-proportioned figure. She wears her long flaxen hair loose around her shoulders or high in a pony tail. A bright smile breaks easily on her attractive, doll-like face and feelings show openly. Sadness drives deeply when she speaks of her father, Lee Margolin, a former insurance salesman, who died about four years ago. 'We were always close . . . so close,' she said with emotion. 'Without your parents to guide your views, growing up is a throbbing pain.'

Being with John obviously helped fill the void her father left, as did the concentrated effort she put into her own tennis. Ironically, her father, who had so often worked with her, never saw his daughter reach the last sixteen at the 1978 US Open where she defeated Dianne Fromholtz.

Born in the same year as McEnroe, 1959, on April 5, Stacy grew up in the exclusive area of Beverley Hills. With Hollywood in the vicinity, she was used to seeing and mixing with the children of celebrities at school and often had a game of tennis with the ex-angel, Farrah Fawcett-Majors.

It was a thrill for her when she was younger to have the famous living all around her, but the swooning soon passed as she recognized how normal they were.

People are awestruck by Junior because of his position, his personality and his ability. They want to talk to him, request his autograph, but few of them seem to sense when it is a good time to approach him. 'It's like me at a golf tournament,' explained Stacy. 'Suppose I were to sigh out loud when someone was putting? And so it is with John. He's just about to take a spoonful of food when someone tries to muscle in.' But she added, 'Though you may not believe it, he does want the crowd rooting for him. I can't understand the audience sometimes, they're so fickle. One minute they love you and the next they hate you.'

Stacy, like all John's friends, defends him to the hilt. Being an international competitor herself, she can sympathize with the problems John experiences on the court.

'Tennis can be really frustrating, and John gets so mad when he plays a shot he's made so often in practice and blows it, or when a linesman gives a bad call in a point he's worked hard for. John says that the maddening thing is when a ball is out – and, okay it's only quarter of an inch out but it *is* out, and you know it – but the umpire misses it.

'Everyone gets mad about these things, but sometimes it gets to John more than other players because he wants to be so . . . so perfect. It's just him. He works hard and gets mad when someone else isn't doing his job right.'

It is hard to imagine that ranting, raving, pouting kid who appears on court with such consistency could really be a nice individual. However, according to Stacy, he is just that. 'We are talking about a really nice, easy-going, even-keeled guy,' she said earnestly. 'He wants to be a nice guy. Deep inside he wants to be everyone's friend. He is such a good person and I get so mad sometimes because most people make up their minds about him through what they see on the tennis court.'

61

He is very thoughtful as well. One year Stacy was staying at her friend's house in Palm Springs. It was her birthday, but John was travelling at the time. 'I suddenly got this phone call,' she said. 'He wished me a happy birthday and then when I got home there was a huge bunch of red roses.'

John has never been flashy with his money and certainly spends very little on himself, tending to look more like a ragamuffin than a multi-millionaire. But to the people close to him, he is generous. Stacy and John's brother Mark were both given cars. Mark's was a TR3. John said his first car was a Ford Pinto which he bought for $100 and sold for $50. He now drives a powder blue, two-seater Mercedes convertible.

McEnroe wears Stacy's gift to him: a gold initial J on a chain.

The young girl from Beverly Hills says, 'John is the closest I've ever been to anybody, and it's the same for him. But it's amazing the things you learn about a person each time you are with him. He is so perceptive. He can sure read a person. He also senses how I'm going to react most of the time. He's fun-loving, although he has lots of goals and ambitions. We appreciate the independence the tennis world affords us, but as much as I cherish my freedom, I also cherish him. It's vital when you're growing up to feel comfortable with one another and that is exactly what we feel. Very comfortable, very much at ease.'

Their natural carefree relationship enables them to go to the movies, an ice hockey game, play backgammon, play basketball in the park near Stacy's home or jog along the beach at Malibu.

They deliberately avoid the nightclub circuit; although Stacy loves disco dancing, John hates it. Her separate interests include jazz, aerobics and gymnastics. 'Otherwise,' she said, 'it's pretty good. We like the same food – Chinese, Italian, popcorn and home-blended fruit drinks. When John stays at my house, my mom goes crazy when she hears the blender going, because we'd throw in frozen strawberries, peaches, bananas and orange juice. She went crazy because we started doing this around midnight.'

'Socializing does not come naturally to John,' Stacy continued. 'He's really great fun to be alone with or in a smallish group of friends. We can have great fun going out with a bunch of people he knows real well, but he's just not the type of person who can walk into a roomful of strangers, stick out his hand and say, "Hi, I'm John McEnroe. How are you?"'

Stacy is an intelligent girl. She graduated with a degree in psychology and has an avid interest in medicine. She tries to keep up to date with the latest in research. So what kind of life could she expect if she and John were to marry?

'Well, we don't plan to get married in the near future. We are both a bit young and still have a lot of learning about each other to do. If we were talking of marriage I'd want to know how much John would want me to travel with him. I see so many wives on the tour travelling week in and week out – and I don't see how they do it because I don't like travelling all that much. I would have to think it was a case of a few years' sacrifice before we'd be able to enjoy things like a home or family.'

Even if marriage is not on the cards just yet, they make sure they get together as often as their crowded schedule will permit.

'We try to see each other at least every three weeks,' grinned Stacy. This can be an exhausting commitment to uphold, especially if you are on the other side of the world.'

Stacy joined John in London whilst he was playing at Wembley for the 1980 championships. She fell fast asleep in the press room while John finished a late-night doubles match. When he came up for the interview and saw her asleep he asked all present to 'keep it down' so as not to disturb her. The entire press conference was conducted in whispers and amazingly she did not stir.

Stacy emphasized, 'He's a real sweet guy, tell everybody that. Okay, maybe he's a bear sometimes, but he's a gentle bear and I love him.'

A school portrait of nine-year-old John (*Rex Features Ltd*)

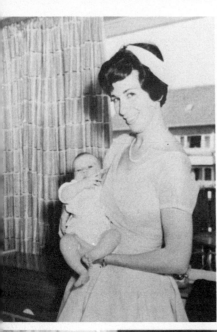

(Left) Kay McEnroe with her young son at their home in Wiesbaden (*Rex Features Ltd*)

(Right) Long-time sweethearts Stacy Margolin and John at sixteen (*Rex Features Ltd*)

(Far right) John winning the Orange Bowl junior tournament in 1977 (*Russ Adams Productions*)

(Below right) Douglaston neighbour Mary Carillo led John to his only title in the French Open, winning the mixed doubles in 1977 (*Le-Roye Productions Ltd*)

(Below) From the family album John with his two brothers, Mark (left) and Patrick, and mother Kay (*Rex Features Ltd*

(Above) John Paul McEnroe, a
New York lawyer, in his Park
Avenue office (*Rex Features
Ltd*)

(Above left) John leaving the
court after his losing battle
with Jimmy Connors in the
1977 Wimbledon semi-final
(*Popperfoto*)

(Left) McEnroe Sr taking up
his familiar position, with son
Mark. With them is Raul
Ramirez's wife and brother
(*Leo Mason Photography*)

(Right) Mother Kay in front of
their home in Douglaston (*Rex
Features Ltd*)

After the United States beat Great Britain in Palm Springs in 1978, the McEnroe family gather around the much-prized Davis Cup trophy with NBC commentator Bud Collins. Later, John enjoys the victory dance with Stacy (*Russ Adams Productions*)

Opposite:
(Above) John and Peter Fleming, the successful doubles partners, win the Braniff Airways doubles at Olympia in 1979, beating Sherwood Stewart and Ilie Nastase (*Popperfoto*), and later that year they took the doubles championship title at Wimbledon (*Leo Mason Photograph*

(Facing page) Life on the tour is not all fun and excitement (*All Sport/Tony Duffy*)

John and Peter, best friends, and doubles partners for the past four years, (above) winning the Island Holiday Pro classic in Hawaii in 1980 (*Russ Adams Productions*) and later that year clowning at the Benson & Hedges indoor tournament which they won (*Le-Roye Productions Ltd*)

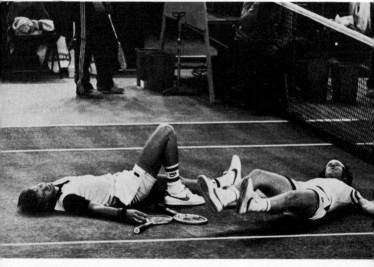

Answering the press (*Le-Roye Productions Ltd*)

(Left) John and Stacy after th WCT finals in 1981 (*Russ Adams Productions*)

(Facing page) The trials of Wimbledon 1981 (*above: Leo Mason Photography; below: Popperfoto*)

(Below) With Madame Tussauds model

(Right) McEnroe and Borg before the start of the historic 1981 final (*Le-Roye Productions*)

(Below right) The new champion (*Tommy Hindley*)

In the quieter moments the pressure is still on (*Above: Tommy Hindley; below: Leo Mason Photography*)

(Left) John joins a jam session with Barry Beck of the Rangers at a benefit for the US Olympic Committee and the Hunger Project at the Xenon discotheque while (below) his parents mingle with celebrities such as Andy Warhol and George Hamilton (*Rex Features Ltd*)

The Davis Cup team celebrate their victory over Czechoslovakia. With John are Connors, team captain Ashe, and Bill Norris, the ATP trainer (*Rex Features Ltd*)

(Above) Borg loses again to the new No. 1 at the US Open in 1981 (*Le-Roye Productions Ltd*)

(Left) Champion for the previous three years, McEnroe loses his Benson & Hedges title to Connors in the controversial 1981 final (*Kelham Pryke*)

Wimbledon

Few people hit the tennis scene with such force and rapidity as John McEnroe. Although 1974 saw the eruption of Jimmy Connors on to the circuit, he was then twenty-two and more experienced in competition. Borg carved his small niche on the pro tour at the age of fifteen and developed his career at a brisk but logical pace. A quarter-finalist at his first Wimbledon appearance, Borg then won the junior title the following year at the age of sixteen. Unlike McEnroe's dilemma of hateful spectators, Bjorn had to deal with thousands of screaming girls who fell in love with his blond Swedish good looks. In '74 he took the Italian and French titles and finally, with the help of Lennart Berglin, his coach and mentor, he manufactured a serve to give him the first of his five Wimbledon titles in 1976.

McEnroe, 'the unknown', however, just exploded on to the green grass in 1977, reaching the semi-finals after battling his way through the tough qualifying rounds. Top, experienced players fell to his ruthlessness: El Shafei, Colin Dowdeswell, Karl Meiler, Sandy Mayer and Phil Dent.

This quick, unnatural birth affected him dramatically. 'All of a sudden it was like everybody wanted to talk to me,' he remembered. 'Where nobody gave a darn about me before. Bang suddenly it was all there, people wanting to write to me, people offering me wild card entries for tournaments, people wanting to meet with me all the time, and the press wrote about how I made faces on court and all that stuff. Well, I've always made faces and shouted. It wasn't that I was being different from usual, it was just that a lot more people got to hear about me. I didn't know how to deal with the press then. Everything really flipped me out. By the time I got to Stanford that fall, I was so tired, so mentally gone, I couldn't face a tennis court for six weeks.'

Shattered he may have been, but Wimbledon he made shake in its foundations. Even though Borg claimed the title for the second year, the word was *McEnroe*. He allowed his talent to flow into the very pores of the lush turf, through the excited nerves of the spectators and the rapid penmanship of the journalists, only to blast them with his criticisms and quick Irish temper into stunned shock. Contempt seeped through the corridors of tradition and 'Superbrat go home' hit the early morning headlines. Henceforth from that moment, he carried the 'spoilt brat' label to every corner of the globe.

In June 1978, after completing one year at Stanford, and winning the NCAA crown, he turned professional. The Rawlings tournament at Queens Club in London was his first competition under this status and John lost in the final to the amicable Australian, Tony Roche. He was watched with interest at Wimbledon after his past performance, but disappointingly lost in the first round to Californian Erik Van Dillen 7–5 1–6 8–9 6–4 6–3.

1979 was a better year. The young American captured some major titles like the Volvo Masters in Madison Square Garden, the WCT Dallas finals and, the Wimbledon doubles title, and reached the fourth round of the singles there beating Terry Moor, Buster Mottram and Tom Gullikson and losing to Tim Gullikson. Both matches against the twins were played on court two, which confused a few of the spectators who had seen John beat Tom the previous day.

Following the fortnight in south London he won the US Open singles and doubles. As fast as McEnroe collected titles around the world, his reputation for bad conduct spread. People who were not interested in tennis were attending his matches to witness the flaring of his renowned temper. The games became rowdy and the officials tightened with expectancy for trouble. The population shouted their hatred for McEnroe with morbid enthusiasm and greeted his court appearances with boos and jibes.

After beating Butch Walts in the first round of the 1980 Wimbledon Championships, he very nearly went out to Terry Rocavert, an Australian who was planning to retire that year. Every available concrete step and upturned bin basket was crammed with fans around court three. Reporters hung precariously over the railings and more tried to squeeze on to the balcony attempting to watch McEnroe struggle in the second nerve-racking tie-break, waiting until the last possible moment before they were called away to file their reports.

John's father surreptitiously left the court mid-way through the duel to the amusement of his son, who later said that his father left to take his younger brother to the airport, not because he could no longer bear to look.

McEnroe amazingly hung on, and finally won the match 4–6 7–5 6–7 7–6 6–3.

Leading up to the final, Tom Okker, Kevin Curren, Peter Fleming and Jimmy Connors fell to the skill and dexterity of the Wilson racket. He plunged straight into the final against four times winner Bjorn Borg, snatching the first set 6–1. An historic match emerged from these two talented performers as they fought in serious contention. The fourth set tie-breaker will be remembered by all with thrill and affection, for each point was an agonizing winner which kept every spectator clutching to the edge of a precipice, including Mariana Simionescu-Borg. The atmosphere was electric and the concentration intense as both players produced some of their finest tennis. Borg grasped seven match points before McEnroe took the set 7–6 (18–16).

Neither deserved to lose and McEnroe, who had walked on court to boos, left with a standing ovation after a 1–6 7–5 6–3 6–7 8–6 loss.

He reflected later about the things which were written on the match. 'Everybody was very positive,' he said, and he was pleased because he felt as though he had pushed himself hard. 'At one point, I started getting a cramp in my foot. Then my knee hurt. But I pushed myself anyway. I felt I did my best. It was, like . . . like I was playing from within.'

The 1980 title made it Borg's fifth, and thus he became a legend in his own lifetime. The only person beating this record was William Renshaw who claimed the cup for six consecutive years, from 1881 to 1886, playing only the final round, not right the way through the draw as is required today.

McEnroe, of all the present-day players, was said to have the ability to defeat the Swede especially on grass with his wide-angled, heavily sliced, left-handed serve. Bjorn pointed out that, 'Apart from his great serve he can also hit a soft ball and then a hard one.' He added, 'You never really know what to expect. He can do anything with the ball, he had so much feel for it.' However, as Chris Lloyd once remarked, 'It takes more than just tennis to win Wimbledon.'

The championships are recognized by all the players of the game to be the greatest in the world. To win is the ultimate in tennis and the subject of many a child's dreams.

As the tennis calendar flies round to Europe, the Italian and French Championships are played, but little notice is taken by the general public. Then suddenly Heathrow Airport spills out young men and women with armfuls of rackets. 'Full' signs go up in the bed & breakfast houses in Putney and billboards advertise the forthcoming events.

The players are actually in England for just over a month, playing in either the Beckenham or Manchester tournaments, then in the Stella Artois tournament at Queen's Club followed by the Lambert and Butler tournament in Bristol.

Queen's has always been a favourite of McEnroe's. The third-time champion claims that Clive Bernstein, the tournament director, was very kind to him in 1977 when he first arrived in England and so he has supported the tournament ever since.

It is the Wimbledon fortnight, though, which manages to touch even the people who know nothing about tennis with that special kind of magic.

As soon as the last ball is hit on centre court, preparations begin for the next championships. Applications pour in for the 'Grand Ballot' of tickets which is held on January 31st. Obtaining tickets is quite an achievement, even the players have trouble, complained Vitas Gerulaitis. Competitors in the main draws receive only one for centre court, every alternate day and one ground pass for those when they are without tickets. There is no facility for them to buy extra, even for members of their family.

Apparently, in 1981 some children were queuing up for 'free standing room' when they saw McEnroe approaching. One of them went up to him and asked if he could take a picture. 'Sure,' replied Junior and then asked the boy if he had a ticket. On being told no, John handed over a centre court pass.

Of all the tournaments, Wimbledon places the most stress on those working within its confines. (A different, almost crazy tension is experienced at the US Open.) Off court is where the pressure is felt. Frenzied discussions take place between players and sponsors in the 'tea room' or with powerful agents such as Mark McCormack of International Management Group and Donald Dell in the elaborate marquees with their chandeliers and red carpets. Journalists from every nation come to report on the action of their representatives and their respective photographers follow. The press room is set up with eight television sets covering the centre and number one courts, plus various ones outside. There are also headphones to pick up the radio broadcasts. An after-match interview takes place at the request of the 'daily' reporters and is transmitted up to one of the TV sets so a reporter can sit all day in the room and miss very little, unlike the photographers who have to fight for their positions every day. Each morning they queue for their seat allocation: courtside, on the platform or in the 'pits'. The latter, more unsavoury place, is in the middle of the crowded public standing room area.

On finals day, some of the photographers will sit on 'platform B' next to the Royal Box from nine o'clock in the morning to secure their place, and then have to work from two o'clock for the duration of a two- or three-hour match. For most, match-point is the shot of greatest importance for the whole of the championships and the tension reaches a crescendo as that moment is neared. One year an excited spectator stood up just as the crucial point was played, blocking the view for several photographers. After waiting nearly eight hours for that picture, it took a considerable amount of alcohol to calm their shattered nerves.

Foreign players tend to think Wimbledon is a little too stiff in the upper lip and too heavily steeped in tradition and, like McEnroe, find acceptance far harder to conquer than the opponents.

The present generation, worldwide, has been fighting old-fashioned rules and establishments in all spheres: sports, like in cricket and rugby for example, also in literature, films and in social attitudes. Even Prince Charles became the first monarch to bestow a kiss on the lips of his bride whilst standing on the Royal Balcony.

The difference between Wimbledon and the rest of the world comes openly into view for the duration of the championships. Quite simply the world is prepared to adapt to the required changes, and the people at Wimbledon are not, or so it would appear.

Once it was a grand occasion to visit the All England Club during the last week in June and the first week in July. High-class women dressed in their finery walked elegantly around the rose-bordered courts, escorted by chivalrous gentlemen. Now, the gates are flung open to the T-shirt and denim brigade, whilst the players are still expected to emulate the roles of their predecessors of fifty years ago.

'But I was brought up to fight for everything,' said McEnroe. 'My father's that way. He gets upset and I'm sure that has a lot to do with my personality. When you grow up in that kind of environment, there's no way you can back out on your emotions. I just can't hide it like Borg. I've accepted that it's impossible for me to do that.' Having recognized that this trait in his character is undesirable to some, he said, 'All I can do is work on keeping myself under control, trying not to be offensive,

71

trying to ignore people who want to bug me. Let's face it, anybody who thinks I enjoy the kind of stuff I go through with the fans is crazy.'

McEnroe's behaviour in 1977 was not so abnormal for an average eighteen-year-old. Even at twenty-two most males are far from mature. Perhaps he seems older due to his early dominance in the game and the amount of tennis he has already played to such a high standard. Some classic matches feature his name and will be noted in the history books for many years to come. He has generated so many headlines and been the centre of so much publicity that it is no wonder he appears a veteran and is expected to behave like one. 'It's kinda weird,' he said, 'but a lot of my friends from the junior days, even college, are starting to show up on the tour now. It's great to see them but I feel like an old man sometimes.'

Training for Wimbledon begins several months in advance. Players build up their stamina for the long five-set matches and endeavour to time their physical programme so that they reach peak-fitness during the fortnight. As John does not like to take any extra exercise, he admits that he has never really been fully fit for the past four years.

The top players get accustomed to the grass by playing in the tournament at Queen's or – as Borg does – practise privately. Those without sufficient computer points to get direct entry into the draw have to play the tough qualifying rounds at the Bank of England ground in Roehampton. Here the players fight for every point; they are not interested in entertaining. They have got expenses to pay, contracts to keep up, and heaven help any umpire who takes a point away from them. Places are kept in the draw for qualifiers and 'wild card' entries, the latter given at the tournament's discretion, usually to British players.

Qualifiers can often pose a big threat to the established

players because they are young and eager to prove themselves and have nothing to lose.

McEnroe's goal for the 1981 championships was to break Borg's long-standing hold on the cup. Their head-to-head record then stood at 7–5 to Borg.

	Venue	Rnd	Winner	Score
1978	Stockholm	S	McEnroe	6–3 6–4
1979	Richmond	S	Borg	4–6 7–6 6–3
1979	New Orleans	S	McEnroe	5–7 6–1 7–6
1979	Rotterdam	F	Borg	6–4 6–2
1979	Dallas	F	McEnroe	7–5 4–6 6–2 7–6
1979	Canada	F	Borg	6–3 6–3
1980	Masters NY	S	Borg	6–7 6–3 7–6
1980	Wimbledon	F	Borg	1–6 7–5 6–3 6–7 8–6
1980	US Open	F	McEnroe	7–6 6–1 6–7 5–7 6–4
1980	Stockholm	F	Borg	6–3 6–4
1981	Masters NY	R/r	Borg	6–4 6–7 7–6
1981	Milan	F	McEnroe	7–6 6–4

S – Semi-final, F – Final, R/r – Round robin

This table does not record exhibition matches, such as their three confrontations in Australia for the Golden Racket tournament.

McEnroe pointed out that his win over Borg in 1978 was probably the biggest game of his career, because it gave him the most confidence. 'If I could beat Borg, I knew I could beat others.'

After his magical final against Borg in 1980, McEnroe returned to Wimbledon hoping that he had earned the respect of the crowd and press, and so would get favourable coverage. Everybody was ready to welcome last year's hero, but he blew the small amount of repair he had made to his reputation in his first-round match against Tim Gullikson on court one. He got fired up over some bad line calls and then coined the now famous phrase, 'This is just the pits of the world', and called the linesman an 'incompetent fool'.

'I thought the guy made eight bad calls in that area, but people tell me I've got to accept it. If someone else can do it there is no reason why I shouldn't, if I am a good enough player; it's just that every time it happens you go "God, I won that point and he took it away."'

'It is the way they treat you, if you can understand that. I hit ten pounds of chalk and the guy says that it hit the outside edge of some small patch of chalk outside the line. I mean, who is he kidding . . . six thousand people in the stands saw the ball hit chalk on the line and he is trying to explain to me that it hit a small patch of whatever it is. You don't treat a player like a kid and then not expect to get treated like a kid back.

'I think I was definitely wrong in what I said, but I felt justified in calling the linesman an incompetent fool. If I am incompetent I expect to be told so. The fact that I was playing badly and not concentrating caused my behaviour,' he added. 'Feeling the way I do is unnecessary and it only hurts me. There is no one to blame but myself.'

John lightened a little when he was asked about a fan who threw her arms around his neck as he tried to leave the court.

'Oh, yeah,' he smiled with amusement. 'Well, you don't really want people jumping on you as you try to get off the court, but that is probably one of the few fans I have.'

'She yelled out that she loves you,' he was told.

'Well, I don't know if I can say the same back to her . . . but I like her a lot!!'

Serious again, John said, 'It is really important for a tennis player to get over that hill at Wimbledon. Everybody was telling me I should win. But at the back of my head was the thought that "Nasty" and Rosewall had never won it. When it is taken for granted that you're going to get to the semis or final, you get nervous and uptight. That was definitely the reason I got upset.'

He received a hammering from the press after that first day of play which upset him to the point where he played a silent, totally subdued and therefore lack-lustre match against Raul Ramirez in the second round and appeared not even to be able to gather up the spirit to try for some balls. Rain carried the match over two days, but it continued in the same mood. The 6–3 6–7 6–3 7–6 victor looked sullen and depressed as he faced the press afterwards.

'Having to play a match and keep my temper was a very difficult experience,' he said wearily. 'I just wasn't in the match, I seemed to miss my rhythm on the service and everything. It just wasn't me in the first two games. I was concentrating but not acting myself and you have to be yourself out there. Certain balls I knew I should go for but didn't. The bottom line is all about winning and I need to find a happy medium. If I get a little angry with myself on court it really helps.'

During the press conference he kept relatively calm except for his bitter complaints about the distortions of the 'speeding ticket' story, where it was alleged on a radio and television station that he was likely to receive a court summons for driving too fast. It was in fact Peter Fleming who was stopped by the police, and McEnroe was just a passenger.

John beat Bob Lutz and Stan Smith, two of the most experienced Americans on the circuit, and then Johan Kriek, to face surprise semi-finalist Rod Frawley. It is in examining this match that one can appreciate fully the pressure McEnroe had upon him.

Under the watchful eyes of Lady Diana Spencer, John seemed to have difficulty concentrating from the beginning of the match. There were numerous small queries which broke the game up and encouraged a noisy audience. In one explosion where the umpire over-ruled his linesman, McEnroe was given a warning for 'unsportsman-like behaviour'. Lady Diana was whisked off to tea halfway through the match, and McEnroe eventually won 7–6 6–4 7–5 after 3 hours 20 minutes of uninspired tennis, although Frawley put up a good fight.

'I played well enough to win a set,' commented the Australian. 'It was my first singles on the centre court and I found it difficult, and also because John takes the return of service very early. It is more difficult to play against him than Bjorn who stays back after the first return. I can't understand how John ever loses to Borg on grass. It is so difficult to win from the baseline.'

The umpire had, in fact, spoken to Frawley about his slowness on court and was told, 'I have thirty seconds to do what I want.' Rod's theory was that if he went out last he would get the biggest applause. 'It was a tactical thing for me,' he smiled.

McEnroe's worst experience of the entire championships must have been the grilling he was given by the press after this particular match.

The interview room was divided between tennis reporters who know the players and understand tennis, and the news reporters who look just for a sensational story in sport or any other field. A number of players would refuse to attend a conference after such a match, even at the cost of a 'fine', knowing that they would be in for a tough time, but all credit must be given to McEnroe for he did not back out. He considers it one of his duties to tennis.

As John sat down uneasily facing a packed room and a table full of microphones, this conversation followed:

You've kept yourself in check for a few days, John, do

you feel you're boiling up inside a little bit?

'Well, you know I've been trying to do just the best I can in the tournament, I mean, you want to get to the finals, that's all, so that is why I was tense, and he played pretty much better than I thought and I needed to take advantage of the chances and when I didn't I just got aggravated with myself.'

Have you and Stacy split up?

'You know, it's people like you that make me sick, you know that, all these papers here write such bullshit it's amazing, it really makes me sick, it's none of your business, first of all and the answer is no, I mean I shouldn't even tell you that because you are such trash anyway, but I'm sure you'll quote me on that, won't you, you'll just quote exactly what you damn well please.'

But you said it, with all due respect!

'I want to say it, I'd like you to quote that you guys are shit. I can't get any worse, the press I'm getting here because you guys are just so low that it makes me sick, man, can't you pick on someone else man, you got anyone else you can pick on.'

Can we have questions on tennis?

'Yeah, don't ask me questions about myself all right, talk about the match.'

John, can I ask one question which isn't about tennis?

'No.'

I'm here to cover Lady Diana!

'Oh, I don't know . . . Ah she's a terrific person.'

The press room at this stage collapsed into raucous laughter, but John just sat with a glazed stare on his impassive face.

But she's English!

'Great, that's just great.'

John, how do you account for the slow play – although

77

there were no rallies, or no noticeable rallies, it lasted three hours for three sets?

'Well, I think he took a lot of time between his serves and I'm not the fastest player but I found someone who plays a lot slower than I do.'

John, did you do something to your left knee at one point?

'I hit myself with the racket on the return, but everyone thought I was stalling . . . I was just trying to walk it off.'

You said everybody but surely the crowd is very evenly divided, you have got some very ardent supporters out there.

'I might have a lot of supporters if people didn't write the stuff that they wrote in these papers. You know people read this and they believe it. They believe that Stacy and I split up, they believe that I got a speeding ticket and just lies and that's all it is. Why don't you write that you lie, can you write that in the paper, write that you're liars? We can't do anything about it, that's the sad part. You can lie all you want to and we can't do anything about it, except get shit on more the next day.'

You could try suing.

'I wouldn't waste my time with low people like you.'

I believe during the course of the game you made thirteen separate complaints. Would you say that each and every one of them was wholly and totally justified?

'I don't even want to answer that question.'

Would you agree that you made thirteen separate complaints?

'I have no idea.'

You have no idea, do you feel they were all justified?

'I have no idea.'

You have no idea whether they were justified?

'I have no idea how many I made.'

78

Do you think those you did make were . . . (McEnroe broke in)

'What do you want me to say . . . that my underwear is purple? Give me a quote and I'll say it for you.'

I'll tell you what he's trying to say, he is saying that you are putting the other person off by your behaviour.

'That's such nonsense. You know so little about tennis if you think that is true. The guy plays twice as slow as I do. That guy was the reason it took three hours, nothing against him, he just takes thirty seconds between every serve, the complaints took two minutes. Half of them I just pointed my racket at and that was it. The guy was on me before I could even say anything. I can't believe the way you people think. What do you think this is? It's sad to talk to people like you, it really is.'

We think it is a tennis tournament . . .

'Well, I wish you'd write about it.'

. . . in which fairness . . .

'Why don't you be fair to me then?'

. . . should be looked after equally for both players on the court.

'And it was unfair that I questioned a call?'

I think that when it comes to thirteen complaints during the course of a match some of which . . .

'Only about nine were one hundred per cent and four were seventy-five per cent right.'

John, putting all this aside for a moment and assuming that you meet Borg in the final, how is your game?

Great question [a member of the news press said sarcastically].

'And yours are right?' said McEnroe incredulously.

Then a tennis reporter shouted across the room to the offender, 'Shut up man, why don't you be quiet, it's our press conference, not yours.'

And McEnroe followed on by saying, 'Why do you

come here, you come just to piss me off, you've pissed me off, are you happy now? You have made your great point.'

Ignore him, John.

'I don't want to talk anymore, all right?'

The unhappy, infuriated American left the interview room amid the arguments between the tennis press and news men.

An apology was later made to John, and the man in charge, Roy McKelvie, announced that the news men would not be admitted into the conferences in future, but the damage had been done.

The *Daily Mail* reported John McEnroe Sr as saying after the match, 'There is no perspective involved. The things they write about involve a few minutes of a three-hour match. They ought to be talking about his tennis, his tenacity, his courage, all those things that make him a champion.' Continuing, he said, 'I have never countenanced unsatisfactory and untoward behaviour on a tennis court. There is no room for obscenity or threatening or outrageous conduct from anyone. But neither do I think there is anything sacred about officials. I think they should be subject to scrutiny like the players and, if they don't do their jobs properly, told to go and find something else to do. The arbitrary and capricious nature of officialdom at Wimbledon is something that John has a problem with and so do I. Generally, though, it is only John's high demands of himself which makes him over-react. Of course Bjorn Borg doesn't do it. But quite simply Borg doesn't do anything. Their personalities are completely different. People shouldn't expect John to be another Bjorn Borg.'

ATP executive director, Butch Bucholz, does not consider petulance on court as a modern phenomenon. 'It's been going on for years,' he said. 'You can go back to the days of Big Bill Tilden, for example. He threatened to walk off courts and do all sorts of things. What's happened is that tennis players have become celebrities and almost have the stature of movie stars. When they do something now it is much more visible so far as the public is concerned.'

John's behaviour may have made it to the front and back pages of the newspapers every day for two weeks, but it was his tennis that pushed him into the doubles final with long-time friend and partner, Peter Fleming. A 6–4 6–4 6–4 win over Bob Lutz and Stan Smith gave them back the title they had lost the previous year. Fleming said after the match, 'I felt bad that we did not win either the US Open or Wimbledon last year, even though we won about eight tournaments.' With a boyish grin he added, 'I will be rooting for John tomorrow. I would even sleep on the pavement to see the match.'

He would not have been alone. People started queuing outside the All England Club three days before the final. The whole country, and much of the rest of the world was alive with anticipation as the stage was set for the confrontation between the number one and number two, Bjorn Borg and John McEnroe.

The Swede had played a brilliant semi-final match against Jimmy Connors, pulling back from two sets to love down, winning 0–6 4–6 6–3 6–0 6–4. If Borg could produce tennis of the same calibre in the final, McEnroe was in for the hardest battle of his life. He had not been serving well all week, and with the pressure of outside matters on top of him, the twenty-two-year-old would need all his strength to block everything out and just concentrate on his tennis. Chris Lloyd had beaten the young, awestruck Czech, Hana Mandlikova in the ladies final 6–2 6–2. So as Chris and her husband John Lloyd happily returned home, all eyes rested on the men.

The morning of the fourth of July finally arrived and small armies of ball boys and officials received their final instructions as crowds massed beyond the huge black iron gates. At twelve o'clock hoardes of excited people pushed their way through the turnstyles and ran breathlessly to find a space in the free standing area. As the minutes ticked away, the brass band played robust songs, while downstairs in the men's locker room, a pale Bjorn Borg carefully and quietly folded his towels. In due time the 'kid' sauntered in, wearing a denim jacket and, wrapped over his puffball hair were headphones blaring out rock music.

On centre court the ball boys were cheered heartily as they walked on in their Wimbledon colours, green and purple, followed by the umpire, Bob Jenkins and the officials, and they in turn by the players.

Mrs McEnroe was sitting in the 'special box' for the first time along with her husband, their second eldest son Mark and Peter Rennart. Stacy had been forced to return to the States because of illness. The row in front held Mariana Borg, Lennart Berglin and Bjorn's parents.

The champion took the first set 6–4, but one could sense his fear of Junior's heavy sliced serve as they went into the second set tie-break, and it was the serving which proved to be the decisive factor in the match. John only missed one first serve in each of the tie-breakers to win the second set 7–6 (7–1) and the third 7–6 (7–4). With McEnroe continuing to mix up the game using soft chips, slices and top-spin lobs, Borg tired visibly in the fourth set. Down 4–5 he served to stay in the championships.

McEnroe netted the first backhand return (15–0), and again netted the return on the forehand (30–0). Borg sent a crosscourt backhand out (30–15), then hit a volley just long (30–30). A clever chipped backhand from McEnroe made Borg net the return (championship point). McEnroe played a wide backhand to bring the score back to deuce, and then with a winning smash snatched his second championship point. Mariana had long since buried her head. Borg's first serve was hit just wide to the centre line. The second he sent to McEnroe's forehand, who returned the ball and moved into the net. Borg tried to pass him but McEnroe cut it off with a shaky volley which seemed to float timelessly and then landed just within the baseline. McEnroe half fell to his knees in triumph and then met Borg over the net for a handshake in which the champion relinquished the crown. The reign of King Borg had come to an end. Cheers shook the centre court as tears rolled down the faces of the spectators. As happy as they were to welcome a new champion, it was heartbreaking to see the quiet but great sportsman of the game leave his court.

John courteously accepted the prized trophy from the Duke of Kent and then paid a tribute to the man he obviously views with much respect.

'I feel great because I so wanted to win Wimbledon, and I feel especially good because I've beaten a great champion who is one of the finest players who ever lived. I couldn't have picked a greater guy to beat, and I'm very proud to be Wimbledon champion.'

McEnroe as always came to see the press afterwards. Laughing, he said, 'As I felt myself go down on my knees I thought, "You have got to get up because Borg always does that!" You've got to give it everything to be able to beat him,' he continued with obvious satisfaction for the way he played. 'A couple of times I said "Come on" to myself and then said, "Don't even do that, you have got to conserve all your energy. Just use everything you have got for hitting the ball."'

When matchpoint was played John admitted that he was a little hesitant on the volley. 'It took me a while to realize that he wasn't there, then I knew it was all over, just a great feeling. I'm not relaxed yet, but as soon as I get out of here and back to my place I'll start getting very relaxed,' he laughed.

Borg's only comments were, 'I think the rivalry between us is good for tennis, but I will be back.'

A storybook ending to a great era was not to be had. Certain feathers had been ruffled, so instead of receiving his due acclaim, a fine of £5000 was recommended.

Several years ago the traditional Wimbledon ball at the Hilton Hotel, where the two new singles champions had the first dance, was switched to the middle Saturday to enable more players to attend. Now a formal three-hour dinner at the Savoy takes its place.

Many tales emerged as to why John McEnroe did not honour this function with his presence. Some said he refused the invitation as a final snub and others reported that the Wimbledon committee had withdrawn it. John's younger brother, Mark, retold the story when the matter was discussed in California several months later. He said that John had been prepared to go and his father had phoned up the All England Club to enquire about tickets. The party included Mr and Mrs McEnroe, Mark, Patrick and three close friends, two of whom were from Ireland. A reply came back from the secretary's office informing them that only five tickets could be provided. Mark said his father then asked if John could just put in an appearance. This request was also politely refused and Mr McEnroe was told that unless John was present for the entire dinner, the invitation would be respectfully withdrawn.

As if to get the last word in, several days later a message was sent to John McEnroe in the States telling him that the Wimbledon committee had decided not to elect him as an honorary member of the club, thereby breaking one of its own and oldest traditions.

He did, however, receive a congratulatory telegram from President Reagan: after all, he won on the fourth of July, the American Independence Day!

Five months had passed when McEnroe was asked if the Wimbledon episode still vexed him. 'Oh, yeah, I'll never forget it. It doesn't worry me that much anymore. But it does bother me that people still ask me about it. . . . I mean, I go to Australia, beat some guy in the first round and they go, "What's the story on Wimbledon"'

The rigorous demands of the circuit allowed him no time to sit back and relax after the greatest win of his life. The next week there was the Davis Cup to play, followed some weeks later by the US Open.

The finals of the US Open was again between McEnroe and Borg. In another four-set match he demolished Borg 4–6 6–2 6–4 6–3 in two hours 40 minutes, making it his third consecutive win. Whether or not it was the death threat over Borg which had been phoned into the officials that caused this undramatic unexciting match is not known, but it did not compare with either of their Wimbledon meetings. Borg left the court rapidly under the escort of five policemen and made an exit from the site soon after, not waiting for the presentation or press interview.

Officialdom

Wimbledon suffers no more in its troubles between players and umpires than the rest of the world – no single tournament has yet got the right formula – but the umpiring given in Australia at the tail end of last year must simply be treated as a joke.

The 1981 series of tournaments in Australia took the players from Brisbane, to Melbourne for an eight-man event, to Sydney and then back to Melbourne for the Miracle Indoor Championships.

Australian Rod Frawley, who is not noted for being outspoken, almost won himself a reputation in line with McEnroe's. Playing in his hometown of Brisbane, Frawley had some bad calls, which, after a few arguments, lost him the match. The officials, therefore, were not exactly endeared to his heart when they turned up to do their job at the Custom Credit tournament in Sydney.

The line judges tried very hard not to fall off their chairs in frozen concentration and the umpire – poor fellow – would be grateful if the LTAA could supply him with an abacus for the next time he is required to count.

After helping him with the score several times, Frawley was again subjected to some doubtful calls through the course of his match against McEnroe. One incident arose on game point when John served an ace wide to the forehand court. Rod remained absolutely motionless, while McEnroe walked back to serve for the next point. The umpire took one look at Frawley still standing there and announced: 'The serve was out.'

Frawley shook his head in disbelief. 'That ball was ten inches in, you just looked at me and called it fault. I was just testing you. That ball was in.'

Unruffled, the umpire turned back to the microphone and says, 'Game to McEnroe.'

'What do you mean, game? You called it a fault.'

The umpire replied, 'You conceded the point, the score is 4–1.'

'I didn't concede the point, I was just testing you.'

By this stage McEnroe had sat down in his chair. Frawley, seeing him, says, 'What are you sitting down for?'

Mac looks up and shrugs, then growls, 'This guys a jerk, he doesn't know what he's doing. You shouldn't be in the chair all right, you're a jerk.'

John then asked for the referee, Bill Gilmour, to come on court, and told him, 'The umpire should be taken out of the chair.'

'Now that's not fair,' Gilmour replied.

'What – not fair? We are trying to play a match and he doesn't know what he is doing. That's not the first mistake, he's made five already.'

The umpire was not changed and Frawley lost the point, the game, the match and the argument.

The point proved by this little episode was that players can sway an umpire's decision.

Vitas Gerulaitis suffered a similar situation in his final against Peter McNamara at the Miracle Indoor tournament in Melbourne.

Vitas lost the first set 6–4, then recovered to take the

next set 6–1. He was leading 4–1 in the third but Peter broke back. At 5–4 Gerulaitis was serving for the match. Vitas had his third match point when McNamara hit a smash that went *through* the net. The point was given to the Australian. There had been some very bad decisions by the umpire, but this one topped it. The man who had just finished his three-week suspension couldn't believe it. He dropped his racket and tennis ball in the middle of the court, walked off and sat down, to the commands of 'Play on, Mr Gerulaitis.' Finally, it was McNamara who had to come up and tell the umpire that the ball did actually go through the net, which was very noble of him as it gave Vitas his fourth match point. The American was still fuming when he returned to the court, mumbling that it should not be up to his opponent to give the right calls. In this perturbed state, Vitas lost match point four and five and was down break point when he drove a beautiful forehand straight down the line. It was called out. Well, any ideas he had about keeping his slate clean after the suspension flew out of the window. He stormed up to the umpire's chair and demanded to see the referee, who appeared dutifully. The ref would not meet Gerulaitis's request to have the umpire and linesman removed, and so the finalist sat down in silent proteşt. Then, as the regulations state in the Code of Conduct, after 30-second delay the umpire announced '15–0' to McNamara, another 30 seconds '30–0'. The face of Vitas Gerulaitis was immobile. '40–0 ... Game to McNamara. McNamara leads 6–5.' The whispering of the crowd rose to a loud murmur as the American put on his gold watch and gathered together his rackets and waited. Peter looked sad and despondent as he sat at the end of the court. 'Game, set and match to McNamara by default,' announced the umpire officially. Vitas stood up, collected his rackets and walked over to Peter with his hand outstretched. His hand was not accepted at first: nobody wants to win a title under those circumstances. Resignedly Peter shook hands with his opponent and they walked off to the boos and discontent of the audience. He was embarrassed to receive the trophy at the presentation ceremony which followed, but in all honesty, he would probably have won the title anyway, because he played some great tennis to pull back from 4–1. It was the bitter taste that most had to contend with. It is not good for the players, the audience, the sponsors, or the officials.

So these occurrences do not happen just to McEnroe and only at Wimbledon. They are happening all the time in every country the circuit takes them, all the players can vouch for that.

Other little idiosyncrasies cause hiccups in a match which disturb the rhythm and the concentration of the competitors, and it is McEnroe's habit of showing people up if they are not doing their job properly which has made him none too popular with the officials.

Whilst playing in the Transamerican Open in San Francisco, John faced Bill Scanlon in the quarter-finals. It turned out to be a very controversial match, but this particular incident took place at 6–6 in the second set. John dragged himself from his chair after the changeover and as he walked to the baseline to serve, one of the ball boys threw him a tennis ball. He looked at it, stopped and then, standing in the middle of the court, indicated to each ballboy to throw the rest to him. Casting puzzled glances at each other they proceeded to do so as quizzical words passed murmurs went around the stadium. The umpire, watching this little charade intently, announced, 'Time warning, McEnroe,' to which Junior chucked all the balls at him and said with boredom, 'Time to change the balls.' The extremely uncomfortable umpire loosened his collar and withdrew the time warning.

Now some people may think McEnroe was wrong for making a spectacle of an official, but the fact is that mistake delayed play for three minutes and broke both players' concentration. Furthermore, when playing an important match the last thing the players want to think about is whether the balls will be changed on time or whether the judge for a sideline will be paying proper attention.

Trust is a big factor in the game of tennis as it is in many sports. For instance, in gymnastics, where a tenth of a point is the difference between a gold and a silver medal, it is essential the gymnasts know the judges are confident in their understanding of the exercises and their degree of difficulty. Otherwise it would be a waste of time trying to reach perfection because they would still be marked 9.5 instead of 10. The judges have to be trained to see what is good, and that is what should be done in tennis.

There has been a great deal of controversy over the lack of training of the officials. Ilie Nastase said, 'It's the only professional sport that does not have a professional umpire. I want to have a pro guy on the line so that I can trust him. I think McEnroe is right. These people are taking money out of his pocket.'

Technique is learnt through experience instead, not training. It is easy to get hypnotized by a rally. You watch a lob go up, arc in the air and then when the player smashes it, there is no way you are going to keep up with the ball going on to the line. You have to learn to judge when the ball is likely to be hit near your line. Being able to concentrate for long periods of time is also a necessity, and not as easy as it might sound.

One official admitted that the umpires should be trained not only in the rules of the game, but in dealing with people as well. They should analyse each individual's characteristics and act accordingly. McEnroe obviously needs to be talked to and told exactly what his position is.

'When I ask a question [the judges] don't answer me,' John explained. 'That's what really bugs me. It wouldn't be so bad if they would just talk to me and say, "Look, you know there is nothing I can do", or something, instead of being belligerent about it; that makes me mad. I get even more upset when people are condescending to me. It affects me a lot more than it should,' he added.

John also gets very upset if the disputes are shared with the whole stadium. He often asks the umpires to keep the arguments between the two of them and turn off the microphone. 'It's embarrassing for the player otherwise,' he explains.

There are no selection procedures for officials (although those on the Grand Prix circuit have to take a written test); it is those who volunteer purely for the love of the game who get the job, which is a wonderful tribute to tennis, but it is unreasonable for them to be expected to stand such arduous tests and to have insults thrown at them. One lady came off court in tears after officiating at a McEnroe match.

It is 'a thankless job', in McEnroe's words. 'I would not want to do it,' he admitted, 'especially with guys like me around.'

McEnroe said it would be a lot better if some of the umpires could travel the circuit more often, and in doing so get to know the players, share a drink and have a laugh. In that way, the players would trust them. Under the present system the officials are lucky if they spend more than four weeks in the year doing tournaments.

John offered to put $1000 a year into a training

programme for better linesmen and was sure that other players would contribute. Unless the players take the matter in hand, John reckons it could be several years before there is any change in the system.

The confrontation between McEnroe and Connors at last year's Wembley final triggered a huge public reaction in support of Junior.

The two Americans, having reached their seeded positions, had the ingredients to make it the most exciting final in the history of the Benson & Hedges tournaments.

The crowds poured in and bought every single item they could lay their hands on if it carried McEnroe's name or, better still, bore his photograph. The stadium became alive as people took to their seats. While the players warmed up, their list of achievements were given over the loudspeakers, and the crowd settled down to watch an epic match.

McEnroe had lost in Tokyo the previous week to Vince Van Patten, the movie star who is doing well on the tennis circuit. Wembley was his last tournament for the year and he desperately wanted to retain his title. 'I'm tired,' he admitted, 'but I don't want to end the year in a lousy sort of way. I don't want people to say, "Well, he is number one but he had a bad end of the year." I think it's easy to just go on and lose early. If I'm not ready to play a tournament I don't think I should appear. But I've been tired and played a good tournament and I've been as fresh as a daisy and just couldn't hit a ball broadside of a barn.'

The final was not an epic. Certainly, it will be talked about for some time to come, but it resembled a battle of the gladiators rather than the game we once knew. There was some good tennis and some bad tennis, with Connors fighting his guts out all the way. McEnroe took the first two sets with relative ease, 6–3 6–2. It was in his service game, down 1–0 in the third set, when he slammed a ball into the stop netting, venting his frustration for losing the previous point. John was given a warning which, in the true McEnroe spirit, he questioned. The crowd had been waiting all afternoon for a moment like this, and all hell let loose as they booed, jeered and stamped their feet, goading McEnroe on. Connors took a seat in the audience and was besieged by photographers, whilst McEnroe argued his case and was made to forfeit a point for attempting.

The result of that fracas was Connors won Mac's serve and the set and went on to clinch the next two, and thus the championship, from the despondent number one in the world, who seemed too tired at the end of the year to fight Connors, the officials and the crowd.

'I think it goes too far because we are so restricted,' decided Jimmy. 'If there was less restriction the players would let up.'

Both players were fined. Junior $350 for racket abuse – he hit a BBC microphone and broke it – and $350 for ball abuse. Connors lost $400 for audible obscenity. The general outcry was that the umpire had been too harsh on McEnroe. He was too quick to give him a public warning for hitting the ball into the back netting, which is, after all, an act seen on tennis courts all over the world at any level and purely an action to relieve frustration and self-criticism. Connors committed the same evil deed during the match, and was not fined. The argument arose that McEnroe's ball could have hit the linesman and therefore he deserved to be fined.

Another problem in the match was that on several occasions the umpire lost the score, which put extra strain on the players as they lost their faith in him. The Grand Prix supervisor was called on with the referee,

Colin Hess, to sort out the situation, thus stripping the umpire of all his authority.

The fines John incurred at Wembley took him over the $5000 limit for minor offences which had accumulated over the year. Automatic suspension followed for a period of twenty-one days according to the Code of Conduct. Although this rule looks quite threatening on paper, it actually did not affect McEnroe's plans in the slightest. The Benson & Hedges tournament was the last Grand Prix event that he intended to play before the Volvo Masters in January. So he picked up some money playing eight-man events in Milan and Barcelona to cover his losses in fines, as the suspension does not penalize him from exhibition matches, and by the time he had to play the Davis Cup final against Argentina it was over.

The Men's International Professional Tennis Council (the Pro Council) are responsible for the rules and regulations of the game. This 'body' consists of nine representatives: three for the players, three from the International Tennis Federation, and three for the tournament directors. Together they form the 'Player Code of Conduct', which is a rule book stating all the incidents for which a competitor can be fined or defaulted during a tournament.

The list covers a wide variety of offences from failure to complete a match down to not being dressed correctly. It firmly states that under no circumstances can the player wear 'sweatshirts, dress shirts, T-shirts or Bermuda shorts'!

The rules are logical and a necessity to the million-dollar game, but there were still difficulties in that individual tournaments were liable to add a few of their own from time to time, which of course upset the players. So in the summer of 1980, six supervisors were appointed under the directorship of Dick Roberson to travel on the Grand Prix circuit, briefing all the officials as to the rules and then remaining on site to give the final decision if the umpire is unable to cope with a situation.

With Dick, there was Kurt Nielsen, Franco Bartoni, Ken Farrar, Frank Smith and Bill Gilmour. They are an unbiased group whose only interest lies in keeping the game on a straight line. It is not for them to worry if the box office sales go down due to the defaulting of a competitor.

The need for a governing body was apparent at the 1981 French Open Championships when an awkward situation – now referred to as the 'French Affair' – arose, involving Manuel Orantes and Guillermo Vilas from South America. The Argentinian did not turn up for his quarter-final match and so was defaulted by the supervisor. Vilas's excuse was that of illness: he had been suffering from stomach pains and made a request for the match to be postponed until the following day. The French Tournament Committee over-ruled the supervisors' decision, not wanting to disappoint the spectators, which in turn incensed Orantes to the extent that he defaulted from the championships. In fact, after this incident all the players became so irate that they threatened to pack their bags and pull out.

Although the tournament was completed, and it was later discovered that Vilas had appendicitis, the wound had been opened.

By the time the players reached Wimbledon, a storm was brewing. Heated discussions took place in the tea room, and finally the players declared they would not play the US Open unless Dick Roberson and his crew were in charge. As the entry deadline came and went, 86 of the top 100 ranked players on the ATP computer had withdrawn or not entered.

The Grand Prix supervisors won the case and the tournament was played.

Unfortunately, the players are now feeling suffocated by the regulations. They are finding themselves losing points or money for throwing a racket down in frustration, or calling themselves names, faults of which even the most virtuous player can be guilty. And it is of course the top, controversial offenders who suffer. Many of the lesser-ranked players get away with far worse.

One of the more recent rules introduced by the ITF state that linesmen must report any offensive behaviour or gesture whether it is seen or heard by the crowd or not. The umpire can then award a penalty or inform the player that it will be brought to the notice of the Grand Prix supervisor.

Tish Kriek, wife of the South African, Johan, said that her husband had been given a warning for calling himself 'a dumb donkey'.

'A lot of things are starting to stink in this game now,' retorted Jimmy Connors. 'They're coming down on the players too much. Players have no control, no nothing any more. They are putting the thumb on personalities,' he continued.

'You tell a guy like Nastase that he can't act the way he does and you stifle his game. What they are doing is forcing the characters out of the game. And if it gets to the point where I, personally, no longer enjoy playing, I'm gone. There are too many other things I like to do.'

Ilie himself said, 'The game is boring and dull and these rules will really kill it.'

After McEnroe's heated ventilations at the 1981 Wimbledon Championships a $10,000 fine was recommended by the Wimbledon committee. This was lowered to $5000 by the Pro Council and John decided to appeal against it.

Four months later, on 20 November the three arbitrators met in New York for a hearing. One arbitrator was picked by the chairman of the council, Judge Robert Kelleher, the other, Harry Hopman, was chosen by McEnroe, and the third, agreed on by the other two arbitrators, was District Attorney Krieger. After the meeting, they took the evidence away with them to study and decide whether John should pay the fine.

Prior to this meeting, whilst competing in the Benson & Hedges tournament at Wembley, John McEnroe made his views known to the press during the post-match conference.

Does this whole business of the fine worry you, and do you think about it?

'I'm definitely going to listen to what the result is. I think it would be a definite cop-out if they voted against me. In my opinion no one has had the guts enough to see that I didn't do what they said I did. You know, maybe if everyone votes against me I might be proven wrong. It just shows the whole system if I lose this. . . . But I've seen it already, so it wouldn't surprise me. I would be disappointed on principle if I lost. That was the only reason I fought in the first place: it's not the money or anything.

'Mr Hopman is a person I have known since I was so little. I mean, I was reluctant to pick him even as an arbitrator because if he voted against me I wouldn't want that to enter into our friendship or relationship we have with him and my family.'

What would you do if that did happen?

'I don't know what I would do in that circumstance. I mean, I guess I would just accept it, there is nothing more I can do. . . . I would be disappointed. You know if he

97

votes against me then something might have really been wrong.'

All the fines from the players go to the Pro Council, don't they?

'That's one thing that really bothers me. I think the players' association should get their own fines. We are in the red from what I heard, like $300,000, so why do they get it? It doesn't make sense, it's just like the whole thing . . . like being suspended. Half the time you don't know when it is going to start – the whole thing is ridiculous. I don't think half the players have any idea what is going on.

'It's so typical, it's unbelievable. You know like Wimbledon threatening to pull out of the Grand Prix if I didn't get fined. That's not at all political, is it? No one knows about the fact that they go in there and say, "Well, if you don't fine Mr McEnroe we are going to pull out of the Grand Prix". That's not a pressure tactic at all,' he said sarcastically. 'They don't even allow people to make their own decisions; they have to influence their decisions. But even that doesn't surprise me.'

Will a solution be found in the foreseeable future? Fines do not really hurt the players and neither, apparently, do suspensions, unless they include the major tournaments or perhaps the Davis Cup. The players, however, cannot be permitted to rant and rave on the court or abuse the officials.

When it was announced late on Tuesday evening of 26 January that McEnroe would not be fined for his Wimbledon behaviour the *Daily Telegraph* reported that 'Harry Hopman had given a *carte blanche* to thuggery on the tennis court'. It emphasized the difficulties the Men's Council and the ITF are faced with in their job to keep the game in line, as it was only Hopman who had voted for McEnroe. The other two arbitrators wanted the charges to stay. 'The rules have been tightened up for 1982,' said David Gray of the ITF. 'The need for such an appeal has been done away with. In future a majority decision will be sufficient.'

Gerald Williams suggested that all the 'bad boys' should be taken off the circuit and allowed to play their own. 'They would make a fortune,' he said.

Money has caused the birth of another serious problem, in the form of a power struggle between the two major bodies in tennis: the Volvo Grand Prix and WCT – World Championship Tennis, directed by Lamar Hunt.

In the past there were around ninety-five Grand Prix tournaments per year, run on a point system. The number of tournament points a player could earn depended on the amount of prize money offered, plus the number and strength of the draw. These were fed into the ATP computer to give him a position on the world ranking list, which in turn determined whether he could attain a direct entry into the draw or had to play qualifying rounds. With the higher ranked players it decided if they were eligible for a seeded position.

The tournaments themselves are rated by 'stars', again according to the amount of prize money and the size of the draw. Obviously the higher the total star rating the more tournament points are available to the participants. The Grand Slam carries twelve points for each event.

WCT was part of the Grand Prix circuit for a period of four years, complying with all the rules laid down. As from January 1982 they introduced their own circuit of about twenty-two tournaments to compete with the Grand Prix, offering lucrative prize money in the hope that it would attract players to Europe, where the majority of the events take place.

In response to this split, a statement was issued by the men's council stipulating the following condition to tennis professionals: for the year of 1982, the players must sign a contract committing them to play ten Grand Prix tournaments other than the Grand Slam events. If they did not, the Grand Prix would refuse them direct entry into the major tournaments, and they would have to play the qualifying rounds.

Vijay Amritraj and Bjorn Borg are the only ones of the top 200 players who did not sign, but none of them were happy with this term. The trouble is, as McEnroe remarked, 'There are a lot of players who don't know the rules, and a lot of things are wrong with the rules. Hopefully, Bjorn, Jimmy and myself will come together soon and try and sort something out, because I do not think it is fair to any player.' John carried on to say that the reason he signed was not because he thought it was the right thing to do, but because he had too much hassle in other areas to break out on his own to argue this matter. 'It's not so hard for me anyway,' he added, 'as I play quite a lot, but for someone like Bjorn it's hard because he is trying to cut down on his schedule.'

Jimmy Connors felt that the increase in tournaments throughout the world would alter tennis for the worse, and John agreed. 'I think there are too many tournaments right now and that this is making it worse, although it will be good for the players ranked between fifteen and fifty, as some of the relatively unknown people will be able to win a $100,000 WCT tournament. But I feel that is going to really hurt the game, and I think that's where we, the players, have to decide it is not the way it should be done.'

So what is the solution? 'Well, I don't know, cut down the number of tournaments and try and make some agreement between WCT and the Grand Prix, because I don't really think its good for the game to have two organizations going against each other. The players have to be together and find an alternative; that is probably the most important thing for us.'

Connors also argued that it was ridiculous having to sign three or four months ahead of the tournament, because when the time came, he might be injured or needed elsewhere, and then he would be fined for withdrawing.

'I don't think we should have to commit for any,' responded McEnroe, 'but that is just my opinion. There is something to be said for having people play certain tournaments, but I know I have supported tennis for the last four years and I don't see any reason why I should not in the future. It really makes me angry that they should try and restrict us, and each year they are going to ask for more and they try to get away with as much as they can. We should have stood up against it this year, but we couldn't all get together on it, that was the problem. I think if it had really come down to it, we would not have signed the rules. We were supposed to meet at the end of the US Open, but everyone went. It's hard to talk when you lose to each other in the semis and finals. Obviously it hasn't been that important to us as a group, but it's going to be. I think they took advantage of the system this year and they are going to keep on doing it until eventually we decide that we are not going to let it happen. For the past couple of years we have just been saying, "Well, it's not that bad," but it's really not that good at all.'

The question of commitment is a difficult one. Whilst the players want the freedom to choose the locations they want to play in, it is hard for the tournament directors to attract sponsors if they cannot offer them any big names.

McEnroe has only been a member of the ATP (Association of Tennis Professionals) since 1981, but has already taken an active part. He loves the game and is prepared to work hard to get it right.

'Unfortunately, not everyone is a member of the ATP,' he remarked. 'But right now that doesn't matter. The important thing is to get the top people together and for them to agree and then to have all the other players support us. I was the one who suggested the meeting at the end of the US Open. I thought it was the best and only time, because we are all going off different ways for the rest of the year. Seeing as I am going to be around for a while and considering my position right now, I think I might have to be the person to take the initiative to some extent. I guess that is part of being number one. If I looked back and saw that I did the right thing I would be happy with myself as I think they are really trying to take advantage of the game. It is only now that I am starting to get these feelings, as the first couple of years I was just trying to settle myself on the tour, but now I am getting ready to do something about it.'

Taking on such a commitment on the part of a player can be dangerous as he is likely to be drawn heavily into the politics of tennis.

'My father is someone who can work on it for me mostly, so I don't have to worry about that too much, but he has his own work, that's the problem, and if he works with me on my stuff, he doesn't really have the time . . . no one has the time. It's hard, I mean take Harold Solomon, I am sure being the president of the ATP has hurt his game. There are other factors but that is definitely one of them. So I think to get involved doesn't help your tennis at all.'

If anyone is capable of bringing the players together, it is John McEnroe. His strength of character and position in the game will be indispensable to the ATP, if he is willing to become the voice of the professionals.

On the Tour

Anyone who is under the impression that life on the pro tennis circuit is a perfect blend of glamour and excitement would be sadly mistaken. It is hard to appreciate how total the commitment to tennis actually is until one follows the tour. For John McEnroe, 1981 worked out like this:

January	8–11	– Chicago, USA
January	14–18	– New York, USA (Masters)
February	5–9	– Toronto, Canada
February	14–15	– Boca Raton, USA
February	23–March 1	– Memphis, USA
March	19–21	– London. Official signing of Dunlop contract
March	23–29	– Milan, Italy
March	30–April 5	– Frankfurt, Germany
April	8	– Fly to Tokyo
April	11–12	– Tokyo, Japan (Suntory Cup, exhibition match)
April	13	– Fly to Los Angeles
April	14–20	– Los Angeles, USA
April	20–26	– Las Vegas
April	27	– Fly to Dallas

April	29–May 3	– Dallas, USA (WCT Finals)
May	4–10	– Forest Hills, USA
May	11	– Rest
May	25–June 7	– Paris, France (French Championships)
June	8–13	– London, England (Queens)
June	15	– Rest
June	22–July 4	– Wimbledon
July	6	– Davis Cup
July	13	– Rest
August	10–16	– Montreal, Canada
August	17–23	– Cincinnati, USA
August	24th	– Rest
August	31–September 13	– US Open
September	14–20	– Exhibitions
September	21–28	– San Francisco, USA
September	28–October 4	– Davis Cup
October	7–11	– Melbourne, Australia
October	12–18	– Sydney, Australia
October	19–24	– Rest
October	26–Nov 1	– Tokyo, Japan
November	2–8	– Rest
November	9–15	– Wembley, England
November	26–29	– Round Robin, Milan, Italy
November	30–Dec 2	– Exhibitions – Barcelona, Spain
December	11–13	– Davis Cup

It was a year spent on aeroplanes, in hotel rooms and tennis arenas, with very little time for socializing and seeing friends. Although they play in all these beautiful locations, very often all the players see are the hotel and the courts. Half of them couldn't even tell you how to get to the stadium; they just allow themselves to be driven to and from the tournament by the courtesy cars.

A hotel inhabited by tennis pros can be easily identified by the washed tennis shirts hanging out of the windows, the piles of rackets in the lobbys and the breakfast room crammed with young men scanning the morning newspapers for the previous day's results.

A few years ago, before money really distorted the game, hotel life was a lot of fun. John Newcombe and a few of the press men can tell some unbelievable stories about the escapades and parties they used to have. Battles with fire extinguishers, midnight swims in hotel pools, and drinking competitions. The Aussies are always where the action is, usually with a beer in hand!

The excessive prize money, especially when it is given in the first- or second-round stages as in the big tournaments or even in the third round, has made players realize that tennis really is a profession in the business sense. So the younger, not so well-known players spend all their time training, not drinking, and making sure they are asleep by 9.30 or 10.00. Expenses are high on the tour, so they cannot afford to lose in the first round too often. Those having to qualify for tournament rely on friendly families to put them up for the week, and where possible they will even hitch-hike to the tournaments. The top players, on the other hand, can afford to stay in the best hotels, but because they are constantly searched for by press and public, they tend to lock themselves away in their rooms, remaining isolated from the rest of the world, and just lie on their beds staring at the ceiling. McEnroe says, 'I am really boring on tour. I never go shopping or sightseeing. I don't even eat breakfast.'

Over the past three or four years more and more wives have started travelling with their husbands. Whilst the first year or two can be very exciting, there is a limit to how much shopping one can do, and unless they are in an exotic place where they can sunbathe, they have to wait endless hours for their husbands to finish matches and indoor tournaments can continue play till as late as one or two o'clock in the morning.

Many couples have started families and travelling with babies demanding a lot from the wife. Hotel rooms are cramped, although those who can afford it book two adjoining rooms, while others have to find space to house all the baby essentials and the tennis gear. Caring for a child out of a suitcase is not easy, and when it is sleeping the mothers can rarely get out of the room, even to watch their husbands play, and at night it is the wife's responsibility to make sure the baby doesn't cry and disturb her husband's sleep.

Very few tournaments have crêche facilities, so the women take it in turns to babysit or some, like Margie and Stan Smith, hire nannies to travel around the world with them. But it is becoming a common sight to see babies and toddlers playing on the club room floors.

Most of the wives cope admirably and bear in mind that their husbands will probably be able to retire from the circuit at about thirty-five and so then they will settle down.

When the Gulliksons bought a house last year in Florida, Rosemary, Tim's wife, was so excited. 'At last, after four years of living out of boxes I have somewhere to hang my clothes,' she said.

Some tournaments do lay on parties during the week, but even these seem to be more infrequent. Perhaps the tough competitiveness of the players is the reason: the more friends you have on the circuit the harder it is to face them over the net.

Practising is hard work too, if taken seriously. As Bjorn

Borg said, if you don't concentrate and work whilst practising, how can you expect to be able to in a match?

In the case of indoor tournaments, the courts are in constant use for matches except early in the morning, so nearby clubs have to be utilized. The pros stand out a mile amongst the local members; they all look the same, wearing T-shirts given to them by various tournaments or sponsors, tracksuit bottoms tucked into white socks and with a pile of rackets on the side of the court next to a giant hold-all which appears to contain all they possess. Courts are often shared so there are always guys sitting around waiting for a hit and cracking jokes. Amazing uninhibited shots are played, which would probably never be seen by the public from that person, because while every player in the top 500 can play extremely well, it is the mental strength during matches that enables a competitor to produce the good shots and the courage needed to play the big points that makes the difference between winning and losing. John usually practises with Peter Fleming or Peter Rennart, but when they are together at a tournament he will practise with Borg and Gerulaitis sometimes.

One of the worst parts of tournament playing is the hanging around waiting for your match. Most of the guys seem to turn up a couple of hours before they are expected to play, so that they can prepare mentally. This just really entails sitting around doing nothing, so that they conserve absolutely all their energy for the match – they even consider reading taxing. If the earlier matches take a long time to complete, they can be there for three to four hours and then perhaps have to wait after their match to play doubles.

Lately John seems to have requested playing his singles and doubles matches straight after one another, with only half an hour break. At Wembley he played for three consecutive days in this format, even to the two finals.

John reaches the final of both the singles and doubles with such consistency at tournaments these days that it is not surprising he feels fatigued at the end of the year, and he finds himself suffering on court from playing too much. 'I hate it when I can't try like I want. When I feel like I'm not there, my mind just snaps. I go bananas inside. I just wanna jump off – jump on a beach or something,' he said.

'For the last two years I've had trouble maintaining my concentration. It is easier for Borg now because he only plays fifteen or twenty tournaments a year so he can be on top form for each event.' After having a good win at a major tournament, McEnroe is finding it increasingly difficult to get himself psyched up for the smaller ones.

The constant drudge of tournament after tournament tires him, even though he is still a young man.

'It's the travelling that really hurts you, that's tough,' he said. 'I get anxious about things and then I don't sleep very well, because I'm not relaxed and that's when you feel bad on the court, because you are a little bit tired or just shaky and it all adds up, it is like a snowball, getting bigger and bigger and then you are edgy all the time. It is almost a mental effort to go out on to the court.' But he admitted that was his fault for committing himself to such a loaded schedule. Every year, he reckons on cutting down his schedule but it has not happened yet. In 1980 he played the much publicized 'Golden Racket' exhibition matches against Bjorn Borg in Australia for three days, then he flew to Memphis, Tennessee, and was wiped out by someone who would normally give him no problem. Two weeks later he went to Frankfurt and Milan, then to Rome, then Japan and finally back to Los Angeles to see Stacy. The trip certainly earned him some money but totally knocked him out.

It is difficult to slimline the year's plans especially with the Grand Prix rules which have just been enforced.

'If you take the ten Grand Prix tournaments and the three major ones, that's thirteen right there,' he shrugged. Any tournaments that John has won, he will go back to the following year to defend his title, and then there are exhibition matches.

Fleming knows McEnroe needs the fix of competition. 'You start out with the fact that Junior's a genius,' he says. 'He's not the type that needs to be regimented. He's hyperactive, all nervous energy. For him, relaxing must be tiring, too – his mind just never rests, ever. I can disengage mine, like a businessman taking a two-week vacation, but not Junior. He puts himself under some heavy strain, he's always out there, on the line.'

One bonus of so much travelling might be the opportunity of learning another language. McEnroe was once asked if he would like to learn. 'I'd love to, but my chances don't look too good if one thinks about the other Americans on the tour. We are not exactly a great bunch of linguists. But I'd like to try. Tennis has come pretty easily to me so it would be a challenge to try something that might be difficult. I reckon I could pick something up if I just listened to a language a couple of hours every day. I'd enjoy it. I think I'd try Italian first. I like that language best.'

McEnroe points out that a bad point of travelling and appearing in different countries all the year round is that the people only see you for a week in that particular country so they do not expect you to be tired, and then they get upset if you happen to be abrupt with them.

'If you walk into a hotel after ten hours' flying,' the champion said, 'and some guy walks straight into you, anyone's going to be in a mood! Also they know who I am and they're going to expect me to react. Even if I say

"Excuse me" they'll go back and tell a friend: "You know what, he yelled at me!"'

'Maybe some people think I'm rude to them. But I don't mean to be rude to anyone. It's just that there are some situations when it's not easy to be nice to everyone. Basically the people who know me, like me.'

ATP trainer Bill Norris travels with the men for most of the year. He stays down in the locker room to look after any injuries they might have or to give them warming up massages to loosen their muscles before a match, so he is very used to seeing the tension and strain the players are really under. In fact, he said at one time the tension became so high that it affected the atmosphere in the whole of the locker room. In an attempt to solve this problem, Bill bought an Easter duck called Clyde! Who could stay in a bad mood for long with a little Easter duck waddling around the locker room!

The public seem to forget that the players go through the same emotional traumas as any other individual. Falling in and out of love, people close to them dying – all these factors can affect their play.

Hank Pfister won a tournament in Hawaii at the tail end of 1981 and as he received the trophy he said, 'I want to dedicate this tournament to my father, who died just after Wimbledon. I wish he could be here now so that I could thank him for all his help. Here's to you, Dad.'

Dick Gould takes the Stanford players over to Kaui, one of the small tropical islands of Hawaii. 'He gets a crowd of people to put up the money so that the players can get a vacation,' John said, 'then we would coach them for four hours a day. We had to get up at eight in the morning and teach, then we would have the rest of the day to ourselves. It was the first time I had been to Hawaii.' Most people might find this island a little quiet as all the action is happening in Honolulu on the island of Oahu, but John loved it. 'It was great,' he said with warm enthusiasm. 'There and Maui are my favourite places.'

In 1980 John played in the Island Holiday Pro Tennis Classic in Maui. Admittedly he only entered the doubles with Peter Fleming because this is one tournament where the players have fun. It is run by Reed Witt with John Newcombe and has attracted some big names over the years, including Jimmy Connors. John and Peter had their girlfriends, Stacy and Jenny, with them and the four spent an idyllic week snorkling and surfing in the tumbling clear waters of the South Pacific, playing golf on the velvet grass of the Royal Lahaina, sailing in the warm tropical winds and drinking exotic cocktails as they watched the sinking sun. When John could drag himself away from the golf course he put in some tennis and managed to win the doubles title with Fleming.

Every year about twenty of them take a ride on a huge catamaran just as the sun is about to slip behind the horizon. Mai Tais and beer flow freely as they sail further down the coastline to watch a Hawaiian torchlight procession. Then it is back to the beach to play frisbee or softball in the dark. The wives love this location and spend endless hours soaking up the golden rays. Tim and Rosemary Gullikson have been going back for the past five or six years and Bill Scanlon knows just about every local on the island.

It has also become a yearly event for a couple to give a party for the players. They throw open their suite at the Royal Lahaina Hotel and the people flood out on to the rooftop balcony to relish the tastes of the 160 odd pounds of seafood they bring down from Alaska: beautiful crab, king prawns, oysters, everything you could think of. So there are some pretty nice sides to the tour as well.

The following week some of the players moved on to Australia while John Newcombe and his crew moved on to Fiji for the Continental Cup, a tournament sponsored by Continental airlines which John states will become the biggest tournament for club-level players in the world. It is a loveluy event run by Dennis McElrath, with its real grass courts surrounded by palm trees.

When John went to Australia in 1980 he stayed only twelve days, but in that period he won four tournament titles and $46,750 in prize money. He won in Brisbane and Sydney in both singles and doubles, beating Phil Dent in the final of the Robinson Classic in Queensland and then went on to beat his Long Island neighbour, Vitas Gerulaitis in the $175,000 Custom Credit Indoor Championships in Sydney.

The Australians loved 'Super Mac' and he said, 'I feel a real friendship with the Australian people. The crowds here know tennis. They are appreciative; they know the time to applaud and that's what I like.'

Another tournament that all the wives and girlfriends angle for is the Monte Carlo Open. The Casino is popular with the players, including McEnroe. The bachelors on the circuit always have a good time here as there are always plenty of gorgeous women around waiting to be noticed. The men's tour is far more exciting than the ladies in this respect. Since the women split from the men's circuit, they see very little of them: in fact they really only come together at major tournaments like the French, US and the Australian Opens and Wimbledon. Whereas the pretty girls will eagerly follow the men around, for the women it is difficult: they cannot go into a bar or disco to meet a man, and very few men will give up their jobs to travel on the women's tour. So the guys definitely get the best deal.

*

McEnroe's loaded schedule in 1981 meant that he had to play Davis Cup the week after Wimbledon, which the Americans won, and then the next major tournament was the US Open where he repeated his Wimbledon success by winning the doubles and singles.

After the US Open John played a week of exhibitions in the States including his day at Stanford. Then he stayed in California for the Trans-American Open in which he lost to Bill Scanlon in the quarter-finals, a match which resembled the one he played against Connors at Wembley. After some heated arguments with the officials he seemed to lose interest in the game.

San Franciso was followed by the Davis Cup in Portland against Australia, and then he flew to Melbourne to take part in an eight-man event called the Mazda Super Challenge. Next week it was up to Sydney for the Custom Credit, which he won, beating Roscoe Tanner in the final. That was followed by a tournament in Tokyo, and then it was to Stockholm before coming to London for Wembley. This was officially his last tournament for the year, and he was complaining of tiredness. But he then flew to Italy to play exhibitions in Bologna and to Spain for the same in Barcelona, and of course there was the final of the Davis Cup to be played against Argentina. It was another victory for the Americans, but still not the end for John. He had agreed to play a charity foundation match which Vitas Gerulaitis organizes, and then another one for Harold Solomon's Hunger Project. A well-earned three weeks' holiday was next on the calendar, two of which John vowed that he would not even touch a racket. On the third week he had to start practising for the Volvo Masters in January and so the 1982 tour took off. 'Three weeks' holiday is the most I have had had in three and a half years.'

Promotion

Within twelve months of turning pro, McEnroe earned in excess of a million dollars, and his earnings have increased sharply with his ability. But he is worth even more with endorsements. Many people feel that the amount players can make is getting out of hand. 'I've always said we get more than we deserve,' said McEnroe in earnest. 'The amount I make is unreal. But as long as you are giving it to me, I'm not going to throw it in the garbage can.'

John says he is really only interested in winning titles now, although he admits he likes the money. 'It is nice to think if you play for five years you may not need to do any more for the rest of your life. But it's winning that is important. It is difficult to know how much money I have made,' he said recently. 'I just give the cheques to my father and he puts them into banks where they can earn interest and all that junk.'

John McEnroe Sr does not take a cut of his son's earnings, although he is a shrewd manager and is doing a remarkably good job of handling his son's career and finances. 'I'm the negotiator and he's the tennis player,' his father said. 'We talk a lot about business deals. I don't tell him, "John, here's where you're going to play this week." I'll tell him what has been proposed and advise him of its merits, but ultimately he decides.'

The big agents like Mark McCormack and Donald Dell have tried for a long time to get John within their folds, as they have managed to do with practically every other major sports personality. But McEnroe Sr holds firm.

'I don't consider myself a power,' he said. 'I'm not an agent and I'm not a promoter. I've gained respect because most people realize that I have no axe to grind, everything is done in my son's interest. I don't get a piece of the action, so I can be terribly objective about things.'

And objective he is. Once he rejected a lucrative beer endorsement because he didn't think it was right for Junior's image.

In 1980 John was offered in the region of $600,000 to play a 'one-off' match against Borg in the black South African state of Bophuthatswana. Bjorn agreed to play but McEnroe turned it down. Instead, he went to Florida to play in an exhibition match for Harold Solomon's Hunger Project. 'After discussing it with my father we both agreed that there was an element of exploitation in the whole thing. I just didn't like the idea of being used to show off a supposedly black state that appears to exist at the convenience of the South African government. I don't want to get into the details because I don't believe in sounding off about things which I don't know much about. And as I've never been to South Africa and have no immediate plans to go there, I obviously can't comment with any degree of accuracy. It was just a feeling I had, call it instinct, if you like. And in any case I am not sure that these challenge type matches are particularly good for the game. It depends on the time and place. Borg and I played three times in one week in different cities in Australia for a lot less money than we were offered to do the South African thing. But I like Australia.'

John is popular in Australia, and during his short stay there in 1981 he did a TV commercial for a local milk, for which he reportedly picked up $30,000.

Although he would not admit to the exact sum, McEnroe signed a contract with Dunlop in March 1981 for around a million pounds to play with the Dunlop Maxply Fort racket for five years. When he was asked if it was the biggest deal he had ever made, he replied with a grin, 'I'd say that's probably a safe assumption.' Did he think that playing with a British racket would endear him more to the English crowd? he was asked. 'I hope so; that was my intention,' he laughed. 'I mean, I hope this year at Wimbledon [1981] will be better because of last year, but I'll take any possible reason to get a few people on my side.'

John has done commercials for 7-Up in the States, and he also has contracts with Nike for his shoes and wears Sergio Taccini clothes.

The truth is John does not need any more money: he could stop playing tennis tomorrow and not suffer. His father, along with Peter Fleming's father, invested some of his son's fortune in oil wells in 1981, and so John is a very eligible young man. Fortunately, he still hungers for tennis titles, and so the world will be honoured with exhibitions of his genius for a few more years.

Every single week of those few years probably will be filled with people arguing for him and against him, people trying to change him and others trying to copy him, but at least he has made the game interesting, talked about and alive.

For John he says when it is all over, he really would like

to see if he has inherited any of his Irish grandfather's musical talent and have a go on the rock scene. According to Peter Rennart, who poured beer over John during his last performance, there's no chance!

'I'm certainly not going to teach tennis to old ladies or play in the over-forty-fives. I'd like to be able to look back on what I have achieved and be proud.'

John McEnroe has already put a great deal into the game of tennis – and one day this achievement will be given the full recognition it deserves.

Tournament record
1977–to date
(See page 151 for Davis Cup)

Compiled by
Alan Little

1)	First round
2)	Second round
3)	Third round
4)	Fourth round
QF)	Quarter final
SF)	Semi-final
F)	Final
RR)	Round robin
3P)	Third place
retd)	Retired
WO)	Walkover

1977

February 14–20
Ocean City International
Ocean City, USA

  1) lost to I. Nastase (Rum) 5–7 4–6

April 19–23
CBS–Virginia Beach Classic
Virginia Beach, USA

  1) bt C. Pasarell (USA) 6–3 6–1
QF) bt R. Lutz (USA) 7–6 7–6
SF) lost to I. Nastase (Rum) 5–7 6–4 3–6

May 6–8
Downeast Classic
Portland, USA

  1) bt O. Parun (NZ) 7–6 6–3
SF) lost to P. Fleming (USA) 6–7 6–7

May 23–June 5
French Championships
Paris, France

  1) bt A. Gardiner (Aust) 6–3 6–4 6–0
  2) lost to P. Dent (Aust) 6–4 2–6 6–4 3–6 3–6

June 20–July 3
The Lawn Tennis Championships
Wimbledon, England

  1) bt I. El Shafei (Egypt) 6–0 7–5 6–4
  2) bt C. Dowdeswell (Rhod) 9–7 6–3 6–1

3) bt K. Meiler (Germ) 6–2 6–2 5–7 6–3
4) bt A. Mayer (USA) 7–5 4–6 6–3 6–1
QF) bt P. Dent (Aust) 6–4 8–9 4–6 6–3 6–4
SF) lost to J. Connors (USA) 3–6 3–6 6–4 4–6

July 4–10
Miller Hall of Fame Championships
Newport, USA

1) bt G. Hardie (USA) 6–3 6–2
2) lost to A. Amritraj (India) 3–6 6–1 3–6

July 11–18
Western Championships
Cincinatti, USA

1) bt T. Noonan (USA) 6–3 6–2
2) bt A. Pattison (Rhod) 6–4 1–6 6–4
3) bt P. Dent (Aust) 6–4 6–4
QF) lost to R. Fagel (USA) 1–6 2–6

July 18–25
Washington Star
Washington DC, USA

1) lost to H. Solomon (USA) 6–7 5–7

July 31–August 8
Mutual Benefit Life Open
South Orange, USA

1) bt B. Nichols (USA) 6–3 6–0
2) bt P. Cornejo (Chile) 6–2 7–6
QF) bt J. Fillol (Chile) 6–4 7–5
SF) lost to G. Vilas (Arg) 2–6 6–2 0–6

August 8–14
United States Clay Court Championships
Indianapolis, USA

1) bt T. Graham (USA) 6–2 6–2

2) bt W. Fibak (Pol) 6–7 6–1 6–2
3) bt W. Scanlon (USA) 6–3 7–5
QF) lost to P. Debt (Aust) 4–6 6–7

August 15–21
Rothmans Canadian Open
Toronto, Canada

1) bt W. Zirngibl (Germ) 6–4 2–6 6–3
2) bt W. Lofgren (USA) 6–0 6–0
3) lost to J. Alexander (Aust) 5–7 7–6 2–6

August 22–30
United States Professional Championships
Boston, USA

1) bt C. Roger-Vasselin (Fr) 6–3 6–0
2) lost to J. Connors (USA) 7–5 2–6 5–7

August 31–September 11
United States Open Championship
New York, USA

1) bt E. Teltscher (USA) 6–1 6–3
2) bt H. Gildermeister (Chile) 7–5 6–1
3) bt E. Dibbs (USA) 6–2 4–6 6–4
4) lost to M. Orantes (Spain) 2–6 3–6

September 19–25
Southern California Championships
Los Angeles, USA

1) bt F. McMillan (SA) 6–2 6–4
2) lost to E. Teltscher (USA) 4–6 7–6 5–7

September 26–October 2
Transamerican Championships
San Francisco, USA

1) bt S. Stewart (USA) 7–6 6–2
2) bt C. Richey (USA) 6–2 6–7 6–3

3) bt M. Orantes (Spain) 6–4 6–4
QF) lost to B. Walts (USA) 3–6 7–6 3–6

1978

January 23–29
United States Professional Indoor Championships
Philadelphia, USA

1) bt B. Walts (USA) 6–3 6–2
2) bt Tom Gullikson (USA) 6–4 3–6 7–6
3) bt M. Orantes (Spain) 7–6 6–2
QF) lost to B. Gottfried (USA) 1–6 3–6

February 22–26
Ocean City International
Ocean City, USA

1) lost to B. Taroczy (Hung) 6–3 6–7 3–6

March 13–19
Volvo Classic
Washington DC, USA

1) bt Tom Gullikson (USA) 6–3 7–6
2) bt R. Lutz (USA) 6–4 3–6 6–3
QF) lost to M. Orantes (Spain) 6–4 4–6 3–6

April 17–23
Smythe Grand Prix
San Jose, USA

1) bt R. Simpson (NZ) 7–6 6–2
2) bt S. Docherty (USA) 7–5 7–6
QF) bt E. van Dillen (USA) 6–2 6–1
SF) lost to B. Mitton (SA) 6–1 4–6 4–6

April 24–30
Alan King Classic
Las Vegas, USA

  1) bt J. Fillol (Chile) 6–0 2–6 6–3
  2) lost to J. Newcombe (Aust) 6–1 2–6 3–6

June 19–25
Rawlings International
London, England

  1) bt P. Fleming (USA) 4–6 7–5 6–3
  2) bt I. El Shafei (Egypt) 6–3 6–4
  3) bt G. Mayer (USA) 7–5 6–0
  4) bt Tom Gullikson (USA) 4–6 6–2 6–4
SF) bt C. Dibley (Aust) 6–3 8–9 6–2
  F) lost to A. Roche (Aust) 6–8 7–9

June 26–July 8
The Lawn Tennis Championships
Wimbledon, England

  1) lost to E. van Dillen (USA) 5–7 6–1 9–8 4–6 3–6

July 10–16
Forest Hills Invitational
New York, USA

RR) bt J. Newcombe (Aust) 1–6 6–4 7–5
      bt W. Martin (USA) 7–5 4–6 7–5
      bt W. Fibak (Pol) 6–2 6–3
SF) lost to I. Nastase (Rum) 3–6 6–7

July 17–23
Washington Star International
Washington DC, USA

  1) bt R. Lombardi (Italy) 5–7 6–3 6–2
  2) bt R. Drysdale (GB) 7–5 6–2
  3) lost to M. Orantes (Spain) 7–6 1–6 5–7

July 31–August 6
Mutual Benefit Life Open
South Orange, USA

1) bt R. Fagel (USA) 6–2 6–3
2) bt K. Richardson (USA) 6–2 4–6 6–1
QF) bt D. Joubert (SA) 7–6 6–2
SF) lost to J. L. Clerc (Arg) 2–6 6–4 3–6

Won doubles with P. Fleming (USA)

August 7–13
United States Clay Court Championships
Indianapolis, USA

1) bt C. Roger-Vasselin (Fr) 3–6 6–2 6–1
2) bt V. Amaya (USA) 5–7 6–2 6–3
3) bt B. Taroczy (Hung) 7–5 6–2
QF) lost to J. Connors (USA) 6–3 1–6 1–6

August 14–20
Canadian Open
Toronto, Canada

1) bt P. Rodriguez (Chile) 7–6 6–2
2) bt R. Hewitt (SA) 6–1 6–0
3) bt H. Gunthardt (Switz) 7–6 6–0
QF) lost to E. Dibbs (USA) 1–6 2–6

August 21–28
United States Professional Championships
Boston, USA

1) bt V. Zednik (Czech) 6–1 6–2
2) bt Z. Franulovic (Yugo) 6–3 6–3
3) bt V. Pecci (Para) 6–2 6–2
QF) lost to H. Solomon (USA) 2–6 2–6

126

August 29–September 10
United States Open Championships
New York, USA

1) bt S. Stewart (USA) 7–6 6–4
2) bt J. Fillol (Chile) 6–4 6–7 6–1
3) bt P. Fleming (USA) 6–4 6–1
4) bt C. Dowdeswell (Rhod) 7–6 6–3 6–3
QF) bt B. Walts (USA) 6–1 6–2 7–6
SF) lost to J. Connors (USA) 2–6 2–6 5–7

September 18–24
United Technologies Classic
Hartford, USA

1) bt S. Docherty (USA) 6–3 6–4
2) bt B. Drewett (Aust) 6–1 6–1
QF) bt G. Mayer (USA) 6–2 6–1
SF) bt H. Pfister (USA) 7–6 4–6 7–5
F) bt J. Kriek (SA) 6–2 6–4

Won doubles with W. Maze (USA)

September 25–October 2
Transamerican Open
San Francisco, USA

1) bt D. Schneider (SA) 6–4 4–6 7–6
2) bt M. Riessen (USA) 7–6 6–0
3) bt K. Warwick (USA) 6–1 6–4
QF) bt A. Panatta (Italy) 6–3 6–2
SF) bt E. Dibbs (USA) 6–4 7–6
F) bt R. Stockton (USA) 2–6 7–6 6–2

Won doubles with P. Fleming (USA)

October 2–8
Island Holidays Professional Classic
Maui, Hawaii

1) bt T. Gorman (USA) 6–2 6–4
2) bt B. Teacher (USA) 6–7 6–4 6–3
QF) bt R. Tanner (USA) 3–6 6–1 7–5
SF) lost to W. Scanlon (USA) 2–6 6–3 3–6

October 23–28
Swiss Indoor Championships
Basle, Switzerland

1) bt B. Manson (USA) 6–2 6–2
2) bt B. Fritz (Fr) 6–3 6–2
QF) bt H. Gunthardt (Switz) 4–6 6–3 6–0
SF) bt V. Amaya (USA) 6–3 6–2
F) lost to G. Vilas (Arg) 3–6 7–5 5–7 4–6

Won doubles with W. Fibak (Pol)

October 30–November 5
Cologne Cup
Cologne, Germany

1) bt A. Maurer (Germ) 7–5 6–1
2) bt C. Letcher (Aust) 6–2 6–2
QF) bt J. Kriek (SA) 6–4 6–2
SF) lost to W. Fibak (Pol) 7–5 1–6 1–6

Won doubles with P. Fleming (USA)

November 6–12
Stockholm Open
Stockholm, Sweden

1) bt P. Larsson (Swed) 6–1 6–3
2) bt S. Simonsson (Swed) 6–2 6–4
3) bt J. Kodes (Czech) 7–5 6–0
QF) bt T. Okker (Holl) 6–3 7–6

SF) bt B. Borg (Swed) 6–3 6–4
  F) bt Tim Gullikson (USA) 6–2 6–2

November 13–19
Benson & Hedges Championships
London, England

  1) bt D. Lloyd (GB) 6–4 6–2
  2) bt T. Okker (Holl) 6–2 6–3
QF) bt C. Barazzutti (Italy) 6–0 7–6
SF) bt R. Stockton (USA) 6–4 6–3
  F) bt Tim Gullikson (USA) 6–7 6–4 7–6 6–2

Won doubles with P. Fleming (USA)

November 20–26
Italian Indoor Championships
Bologna, Italy

  1) bt J. Hayes (USA) 6–1 6–2
  2) bt E. Teltscher (USA) 6–3 4–6 6–4
QF) bt K. Meiler (Germ) 6–3 6–4
SF) lost to P. Fleming (USA) 4–6 1–6

Won doubles with P. Fleming (USA)

December 11–17
WCT Challenge Cup
Montego Bay, Jamaica

RR) bt I. Nastase (Rum) 6–5 3–6 6–4
       lost to P. Fleming (USA) 5–6 6–4 4–6
       lost to R. Stockton (USA) 4–6 2–6

1979

January 3–7
Braniff Airways World Doubles Championship
London, England

Won doubles with P. Fleming (USA)

January 10–14
Colgate Grand Prix Masters
New York, USA

RR) bt A. Ashe (USA) 6–3 6–1
      bt J. Connors (USA) 7–5 3–0 retd
      bt H. Solomon (USA) 6–3 6–2
SF) bt E. Dibbs (USA) 6–1 6–4
  F) bt A. Ashe (USA) 6–7 6–3 7–5

Won doubles with P. Fleming (USA)

January 22–28
United States Professional Indoor Championships
Philadelphia, USA

  1) a bye
  2) bt S. Smith (USA) 7–5 6–1
  3) bt H. Pfister (USA) 6–2 7–6
QF) lost to R. Tanner (USA) 6–7 2–6

January 29–February 4
United Virginia Bank Classic
Richmond, USA

  1) bt J. Bailey (USA) 6–4 6–3
  2) bt D. Joubert (SA) 6–2 6–1
QF) bt I. Nastase (Rum) 6–3 3–6 6–2
SF) lost to B. Borg (Swed) 6–4 6–7 3–6

Won doubles with B. Gottfried (USA)

February 9–11
Pepsi Grand Slam
Boca Raton, USA

SF) lost to J. Connors (USA) 3–6 4–6
3P) bt G. Vilas (Arg) 6–4 6–2

February 12–18
Volvo Tennis Games
Palm Springs, USA

1) bt Tom Gullikson (USA) 6–4 6–3
2) lost to E. Teltscher (USA) 7–6 5–7 6–7

March 19–25
New Orleans Festival of Tennis
New Orleans, USA

1) bt H. Hoyt (USA) 6–3 6–2
2) bt K. Warwick (Aust) 6–4 6–2
QF) bt T. Smid (Czech) 6–2 3–6 6–3
SF) bt B. Borg (Swed) 5–7 6–1 7–6
F) bt R. Tanner (USA) 6–4 6–2

Won doubles with P. Fleming (USA)

March 26–April 1
Ramazzotti Cup
Milan, Italy

1) bt A. Jarrett (GB) 4–6 6–1 6–2
2) bt C. Mottram (GB) 6–4 6–4
QF) bt A. Pattison (Rhod) 6–1 6–3
SF) bt V. Gerulaitis (USA) 6–0 6–3
F) bt J. Alexander (Aust) 6–4 6–3

Won doubles with P. Fleming (USA)

April 2–8
ABN World Tennis Tournament
Rotterdam, Holland

1) bt H. Gunthardt (Switz) 6–2 6–1
2) bt G. Mayer (USA) 6–4 6–1
QF) bt W. Fibak (Pol) 6–3 6–1
SF) bt V. Amritraj (Ind) 6–0 6–3
F) lost to B. Borg (Swed) 4–6 2–6

Won doubles with P. Fleming (USA)

April 16–22
Smythe Grand Prix
San Jose, USA

1) bt J. Sadri (USA) 6–3 7–6
2) bt T. Moor (USA) 6–2 6–2
QF) bt W. Scanlon (USA) 6–7 7–5 6–4
SF) bt B. Walts (USA) 6–4 6–4
F) bt P. Fleming (USA) 7–6 7–6

Won doubles with P. Fleming (USA)

April 23–29
Alan King/Caesars Palace Classic
Las Vegas, USA

1) bt A. Mayer (USA) 6–3 6–3
2) bt C. Barazzutti (Italy) 6–3 6–1
QF) bt J. Kriek (SA) 6–3 6–3
SF) lost to J. Connors (USA) 5–7 4–6

May 1–6
WCT Finals
Dallas, USA

1) bt J. Alexander (Aust) 6–4 6–0 6–2
SF) bt J. Connors (USA) 6–1 6–4 6–4
F) bt B. Borg (Swed) 7–5 4–6 6–2 7–6

May 15–21
Gunze World International
Tokyo, Japan
QF) lost to P. DuPre (USA) 6–7 2–3 retd

June 11–17
Stella Artois
London, England
  1) bt C. Pasarell (USA) 6–4 6–4
  2) bt J. James (Aust) 3–6 6–3 6–2
  3) bt V. Amritraj (India) 7–6 6–1
QF) bt A. Mayer (USA) 3–6 6–2 6–4
SF) bt R. Tanner (USA) 6–4 7–5
  F) bt V. Pecci (Para) 6–7 6–1 6–1

June 25–July 7
The Lawn Tennis Championships
Wimbledon, England
  1) bt T. Moor (USA) 7–5 6–1 6–4
  2) bt C. Mottram (USA) 6–7 6–2 7–6 6–2
  3) bt Tom Gullikson (USA) 6–4 6–4 7–6
  4) lost to Tim Gullikson 4–6 2–6 4–6

Won doubles with P. Fleming (USA)

July 9–15
Forest Hills Invitational
New York, USA

RR) lost to V. Pecci (Para) 6–3 5–7 6–7
     bt J. Alexander (Aust) 6–3 6–0
     bt V. Amritraj (India) 6–2 1–6 6–1

Won doubles with P. Fleming (USA)

July 29–August 5
Mutual Benefit Life
South Orange, USA

 1) bt D. Carter (Aust) 6–3 6–1
 2) bt J. James (Aust) 6–2 6–4
QF) bt C. Kachel (Aust) 6–1 6–3
SF) bt J. Lapidus (USA) 6–2 6–1
 F) bt J. Lloyd (GB) 6–7 6–4 6–0

Won doubles with P. Fleming (USA)

August 6–12
United States Open Clay Court Championships
Indianapolis, USA

 1) bt M. Cahill (USA) 7–5 6–1
 2) bt R. Krishnan (India) 6–4 6–1
 3) bt R. Ycaza (Ecu) 6–1 6–1
QF) bt M. Orantes (Spain) 6–3 6–3
SF) lost to G. Vilas (Arg) 4–6 5–7

Won doubles with G. Mayer (USA)

August 13–19
Players International
Toronto, Canada

 1) bt J. Hrebec (Czech) 6–3 6–2
 2) bt J. Kodes (Czech) 7–5 6–3
 3) bt T. Smid (Czech) 6–3 6–0
QF) bt W. Fibak (Pol) 6–1 6–3
SF) bt V. Gerulaitis (USA) 6–3 6–3
 F) lost to B. Borg (Swed) 3–6 3–6

Won doubles with P. Fleming (USA)

134

August 28–September 9
United States Open
New York, USA

1) bt P. Slozil (Czech) 6–1 6–2 6–4
2) bt I. Nastase (Rum) 6–4 4–6 6–3 6–2
3) bt J. Lloyd (GB) w.o.
4) bt. T. Gorman (USA) 6–2 6–4 6–1
QF) bt E. Dibbs (USA) 2–1 retd
SF) bt J. Connors (USA) 6–3 6–3 7–5
F) bt V. Gerulaitis (USA) 7–5 6–3 6–3

Won doubles with P. Fleming (USA)

September 17–23
Jack Kramer Open
Los Angeles, USA

1) a bye
2) bt F. Taygan (USA) 6–2 1–6 6–1
3) bt Tim Gullikson (USA) 6–3 6–4
QF) bt G. Mayer (USA) 6–2 6–1
SF) bt E. Teltscher (USA) 6–2 6–3
F) lost to P. Fleming (USA) 4–6 4–6

September 24–30
Transamerican Open
San Francisco, USA

1) a bye
2) bt D. Schneider (SA) 6–2 6–4
3) bt J. Sadri (USA) 6–4 5–7 6–4
QF) bt B. Walts (USA) 3–6 7–6 6–4
SF) bt Tim Gullikson (USA) 6–2 6–4
F) bt P. Fleming (USA) 4–6 7–5 6–2

Won doubles with P. Fleming (USA)

135

November 5–11
Stockholm Open
Stockholm, Sweden

  1) bt S. Glickstein (Isr) 6–0 3–6 6–3
  2) bt F. Buehning (USA) 4–6 6–2 6–2
  3) bt S. Docherty (USA) 6–1 6–3
QF) bt N. Saviano (USA) 6–1 6–4
SF) bt W. Fibak (Pol) 6–4 7–5
  F) bt G. Mayer (USA) 6–7 6–3 6–3

Won doubles with P. Fleming (USA)

November 12–18
Benson & Hedges Championships
London, England.

  1) bt J. Lloyd (GB) 6–4 6–1
  2) bt R. Drysdale (GB) 6–2 6–2
QF) bt W. Fibak (Pol) 6–2 6–1
SF) bt G. Ocleppo (Italy) 6–3 6–0
  F) bt H. Solomon (USA) 6–3 6–4 7–5

Won doubles with P. Fleming (USA)

November 19–25
Italian Indoor Championships
Bologna, Italy

  1) bt J. Andrew (Ven) 6–3 6–3
  2) bt C. Roger-Vasselin (Fr) 6–2 6–0
QF) bt S. Birner (Czech) 6–3 6–2
SF) lost to B. Walts (USA) 4–6 7–6 3–6

Won doubles with P. Fleming (USA)

136

1980

January 9–13
Colgate Grand Prix Masters
New York, USA

RR) bt H. Solomon (USA) 6–3 7–5
     bt G. Vilas (Arg) 6–2 6–3
     lost to V. Gerulaitis (USA) 6–3 6–7 6–7
SF) lost to B. Borg (Swed) 7–6 3–6 6–7
3P) bt J. Connors (USA) w.o.

Won doubles with P. Fleming (USA)

January 21–27
United States Professional Indoor Championships
Philadelphia, USA

  1) bt B. Teacher (USA) 6–4 6–3
  2) bt C. Mottram (GB) 6–2 6–2
  3) bt Tim Gullikson (USA) 6–4 6–2
QF) bt J. L. Clerc (Arg) 6–2 4–6 6–1
SF) bt J. Sadri (USA) 7–6 4–6 6–1 6–3
  F) lost to J. Connors (USA) 3–6 6–2 3–6 6–3 4–6

Won doubles with P. Fleming (USA)

January 28–February 3
United Virginia Bank Classic
Richmond, USA

  1) bt M. Cahill (USA) 7–6 6–3
  2) bt H. Pfister (USA) 6–1 6–2
QF) bt W. Fibak (Pol) 6–4 7–5
SF) bt V. Amaya (USA) 6–3 3–6 6–3
  F) bt R. Tanner (USA) 6–1 6–2

February 8–10
Pepsi Grand Slam
Boca Raton, USA

SF) lost to V. Gerulaitis (USA) 6–7 3–6
3P) bt G. Vilas 8–7

February 28–March 2
United States National Indoor Championships
Memphis, USA

1) bt B. Bertram (SA) 2–1 retd
2) bt F. Taygan (USA) 0–6 6–4 6–1
3) bt B. Gottfried (USA) 6–3 6–3
QF) bt R. Lutz 2–6 6–0 6–1
SF) bt B. Mitton (SA) 7–6 6–0
F) bt J. Connors (USA) 7–6 7–6

Won doubles with B. Gottfried (USA)

March 17–23
Frankfurt Cup
Frankfurt, Germany

1) lost to R. Gehring (Germ) w.o.

March 24–30
Ramazzotti Cup
Milan, Italy

1) bt I. Nastase (Rum) 6–1 6–4
2) bt T. Smid (Czech) 6–3 6–2
QF) bt A. Pattison (Zim) 7–6 6–3
SF) bt I. Lendl (Czech) 6–3 1–6 6–2
F) bt V. Amritraj (India) 6–1 6–4

Won doubles with P. Fleming (USA)

138

March 31–April 6
Monte Carlo Volvo Open
Monte Carlo, Monaco

1) bt K. Warwick (Aust) 6–2 6–2
2) bt C. Barazzutti (Italy) 6–1 0–6 6–2
QF) lost to G. Vilas 1–6 4–6

April 21–27
Alan King Classic
Las Vegas, USA

1) bt S. Smith (USA) 6–3 3–6 7–6
2) bt P. McNamee (Aust) 6–4 3–6 6–3
QF) lost to H. Solomon (USA) 4–6 1–6

April 28–May 4
WCT Finals
Dallas, USA

1) bt H. Gunthardt (Switz) 6–2 6–1 6–0
SF) bt J. Kriek (SA) 6–4 4–6 7–6 6–3
F) lost to J. Connors (USA) 6–2 6–7 1–6 2–6

May 5–11
WCT Tournament of Champions
New York, USA

1) bt B. Walts (USA) 6–2 6–1
2) bt T. Moor (USA) 6–1 6–2
QF) bt B. Teacher (USA) 6–1 6–2
S) bt R. Ramirez (Mex) 6–3 6–4
F) lost to V. Gerulaitis (USA) 6–2 2–6 0–6

Won doubles with P. Fleming (USA)

May 26–June 4
French Championships
Paris, France

1) bt P. Dominguez (Fr) 7–6 6–0 6–0

2) bt P. Hjertquist (Swed) 6–4 7–6 6–0
3) lost to P. McNamee (Aust) 6–7 7–6 6–7 6–7

June 9–15
Stella Artois
London, England

1) bt T. Leonard (USA) 6–3 6–4
2) bt P. McNamee (Aust) 6–4 7–5
3) bt B. Gottfried (USA) 7–6 7–6
QF) bt V. Amritraj (India) 6–2 6–2
SF) bt V. Pecci (Para) 6–4 6–0
F) bt K. Warwick (Aust) 6–3 6–1

June 23–July 3
The Lawn Tennis Championships
Wimbledon, England

1) bt B. Walts (USA) 6–3 6–3 6–0
2) bt T. Rocavert (Aust) 4–6 7–5 6–7 7–6 6–3
3) bt T. Okker (Holl) 6–0 7–6 6–1
4) bt K. Curren (USA) 7–5 7–6 7–6
QF) bt P. Fleming (USA) 6–3 6–2 6–2
SF) bt J. Connors (USA) 6–3 3–6 6–3 6–4
F) lost to B. Borg (Swed) 6–1 5–7 3–6 7–6 6–8

July 28–August 3
Mutual Benefit Life Open
South Orange, USA

1) bt J. Lapidus (USA) 4–6 6–3 6–4
2) bt J. Lloyd (GB) 6–0 6–1
QF) bt V. Winitsky (USA) 6–3 4–6 6–0
SF) bt D. Carter (Aust) 6–1 6–2
F) lost to J. L. Clerc (Arg) 3–6 2–6

Won doubles with W. Maze (USA)

August 11–17
Players International
Toronto, Canada

1) bt M. Wosternholme (Can) 6–0 6–4
2) lost to E. van Dillen (USA) 4–3 retd

August 18–24
Atlanta Journal Constitution Open
Atlanta, USA

1) lost to J. Austin (USA) 6–7 4–7

August 26–September 7
United States Open Championships
New York, USA

1) bt C. Roger-Vasselin (Fr) 6–3 6–4 6–1
2) bt S. Krulevitz (USA) 7–6 6–0 6–2
3) bt R. Meyer (USA) 6–1 6–1 4–6 6–2
4) bt P. Portes (Fr) 6–2 6–4 6–2
QF) bt I. Lendl (Czech) 4–6 6–3 6–2 7–5
SF) bt J. Connors (USA) 6–4 5–7 0–6 6–3 7–6
F) bt B. Borg (Swed) 7–6 6–1 6–7 5–7 6–4

September 22–28
Transamerican Open
San Francisco, USA

1) a bye
2) bt S. Stewart (USA) 6–2 6–2
3) bt V. Amritraj (India) 6–4 6–3
QF) lost to J. Kriek (SA) 6–7 3–6

Won doubles with P. Fleming (USA)

September 29–October 5
Island Holidays Professional Classic
Maui, Hawaii

Won doubles with P. Fleming (USA)

October 6–12
Robinsons Classic
Brisbane, Australia

  1) bt M. Mitchell (USA) 6–3 6–1
  2) bt A. Kohlberg (USA) 6–4 6–2
QF) bt C. Delaney (USA) 6–1 6–1
SF) bt R. Frawley (Aust) 4–6 6–1 6–4
  F) bt P. Dent (Aust) 6–3 6–4

Won doubles with M. Mitchell (USA)

October 13–19
Custom Credit Indoor
Sydney, Australia

  1) bt A. Mayer (USA) 6–3 6–3
  2) bt R. Frawley (Aust) 6–1 6–2
QF) bt Tim Gullikson (USA) 6–2 6–4
SF) bt J. Kriek (SA) 6–4 6–4
  F) bt V. Gerulaitis (USA) 6–3 6–4 7–5

Won doubles with P. Fleming (USA)

November 4–10
Stockholm Open
Stockholm, Sweden

  1) bt B. Taroczy (Hung) 6–3 6–0
  2) bt P. McNamee (Aust) 6–2 6–4
QF) bt H. Simonsson (Swed) 7–5 6–3
SF) bt R. Lutz (USA) 6–3 6–3
  F) lost to B. Borg (Swed) 3–6 4–6

November 11–16
Benson & Hedges Championships
London, England

  1) bt T. Waltke (USA) 6–1 6–1

2) bt R. Lutz (USA) 6–2 6–1
QF) bt R. Meyer (USA) 6–3 6–3
SF) bt H. Solomon (USA) 6–3 6–2
 F) bt G. Mayer (USA) 6–4 6–3 6–3

Won doubles with P. Fleming (USA)

November 27–30
Brooklyn Masters
Milan, Italy

RR) bt H. Solomon (USA) 6–2 6–1
        bt E. Teltscher (USA) 6–4 7–6
        lost to G. Mayer (USA) 4–6 3–6
3P) bt Y. Noah (Fr) 6–4 6–3

December 9–14
WCT Challenge Cup
Montreal, Canada

RR) bt W. Fibak (Pol) 6–3 6–1
        bt V. Amritraj (India) 6–3 6–2
        bt I. Nastase (Rum) 6–0 6–3
SF) bt E. Teltscher (USA) 2–6 7–6 6–2
 F) bt V. Amritraj (India) 6–1 6–2 6–1

December 9–14
WCT Challenge Cup
Montreal, Canada

RR) bt W. Fibak (Pol) 6–3 6–1
        bt V. Amritraj (India) 6–3 6–2
        bt I. Nastase (Rum) 6–0 6–3
SF) bt E. Teltscher (USA) 2–6 7–6 6–2
 F) bt V. Amritraj (India) 6–1 6–2 6–1

143

1981

January 8–11
Challenge of Champions
Chicago, USA

RR) bt E. Teltscher (USA) 5–7 6–3 7–6
   bt V. Gerulaitis (USA) 6–3 6–3
   bt P. Fleming (USA) 7–6 7–5
SF) bt R. Tanner (USA) 6–3 6–1
 F) bt J. Connors (USA) 6–2 6–4 6–1

January 14–18
Volvo Grand Prix Masters
New York, USA

RR) lost to G. Mayer (USA) 6–3 6–7 2–6
   lost to B. Borg (Swed) 4–6 7–6 6–7
   lost to J. L. Clerc (Arg) 3–6 0–6

Won doubles with P. Fleming (USA)

February 5–9
Molson Challenge Cup
Toronto, Canada

RR) bt I. Nastase (Rum) 6–1 2–0 disq.
   bt J. Kriek (SA) 6–4 3–6 6–3
   bt V. Gerulaitis (USA) 6–3 6–3
SF) bt B. Borg (Swed) 6–3 3–6 7–6
 F) lost to V. Gerulaitis (USA) 4–6 4–6

February 14–15
Pepsi Grand Slam
Boca Raton, USA

SF) bt B. Teacher (USA) 6–3 6–1
 F) bt G. Vilas (Arg) 6–7 6–4 6–0

February 23–March 1
United States National Indoor Championships
Memphis, USA

1) lost to T. Waltke (USA) 3–6 4–6

March 23–29
Cuore Cup
Milan, Italy

1) bt R. Ramirez (Max) 7–6 6–4
2) bt H. Gunthardt (Switz) 6–2 6–3
QF) bt V. Amritraj (India) 6–3 5–7 6–2
SF) bt A. Mayer (USA) 6–3 6–4
F) bt B. Borg (Swed) 7–6 6–4

March 30–April 5
Trevira Cup
Frankfurt, Germany

1) bt C. Mottram (GB) 6–3 6–3
2) bt P. Portes (Fr) 6–1 6–0
QF) bt B. Teacher (USA) 6–7 6–4 6–2
SF) bt S. Smith (USA) 6–2 6–1
F) bt T. Smid (Czech) 6–2 6–3

April 14–20
Jack Kramer Open
Los Angeles, USA

1) bt F. Taygan (USA) 6–1 6–3
2) bt J. Austin (USA) 6–3 6–2
QF) bt S. Smith (USA) 6–2 6–3
SF) bt W. Scanlon (USA) 6–3 6–3
F) bt A. Mayer (USA) 6–7 6–3 6–3

Won doubles with F. Taygan (USA)

April 20–26
Alan King Classic
Las Vegas, USA

Won doubles with P. Fleming (USA)

April 29–May 3
WCT Finals
Dallas, USA

1) bt A. Mayer (USA) 7–5 6–4 6–3
SF) bt B. Gottfried (USA) 6–3 6–4 6–1
F) bt J. Kriek (SA) 6–1 6–2 6–4

May 4–10
WCT Tournament of Champions
New York, USA

1) a bye
2) lost to C. Kirmayr (Brz) 7–5 6–7 2–6

Won doubles with P. Fleming (USA)

May 25–June 7
French Championships
Paris, France

1) bt V. Van Patten (USA) 6–3 6–0 6–4
2) bt J. Fillol (Chile) 6–3 6–0 6–2
3) bt D. Perez (Urug) 6–1 2–6 6–0 6–4
4) bt R. Ycazo (Ecu) 6–3 6–4 6–4
QF) lost to I. Lendl (Czech) 4–6 4–6 5–7

June 8–13
Stella Artois
London, England

1) bt J. Feaver (GB) 6–1 6–2
2) bt M. Edmondson (Aust) 6–3 6–3

146

3) bt W. Scanlon (USA) 6–3 6–2
QF) bt H. Pfister (USA) 6–2 7–5
SF) bt B. Teacher (USA) 6–3 6–4
  F) bt B. Gottfried (USA) 7–6 7–5

June 22–July 4
The Lawn Tennis Championships
Wimbledon, England

  1) bt Tom Gullikson (USA) 7–6 7–5 6–3
  2) bt R. Ramirez (Mex) 6–3 6–7 6–3 7–6
  3) bt R. Lutz (USA) 6–4 6–0 6–0
  4) bt S. Smith (USA) 7–5 3–6 6–1 6–2
QF) bt J. Kriek (SA) 6–1 7–6 6–1
SF) bt R. Frawley (Aust) 7–6 6–4 7–5
  F) bt B. Borg (Swed) 4–6 7–6 7–6 6–4

Won doubles with P. Fleming (USA)

August 10–16
Players International
Montreal, Canada

  1) bt P. Hjertquist (Swed) 6–3 6–2
  2) bt P. Fleming (USA) 6–3 6–2
  3) lost to V. Amritraj (India) 7–5 6–7 1–6

August 17–23
ATP Championships
Cincinnati, USA

  1) bt S. Glickstein (Isr) 6–4 6–0
  2) bt M. Cahill (USA) 6–3 6–0
  3) bt B. Gottfried (USA) 6–3 6–2
QF) bt R. Lutz (USA) 1–6 6–3 6–2
SF) bt R. Ramirez (Mex) 7–6 6–1
  F) bt C. Lewis (NZ) 6–3 6–4

Won doubles with F. Taygan (USA)

August 31–September 13
United States Open Championships
New York, USA

1) bt J. Nunez (Chile) 6–7 6–1 6–3 6–2
2) bt Tom Gullikson (USA) 6–3 6–1 6–3
3) bt P. DuPre (USA) 6–3 6–2 6–3
4) bt K. Curren (SA) 7–5 6–0 6–1
QF) bt R. Krishnan (India) 6–7 7–6 6–4 6–2
SF) bt V. Gerulaitis (USA) 5–7 6–3 6–2 4–6 6–3
F) bt B. Borg (Swed) 4–6 6–2 6–4 6–3

Won doubles with P. Fleming (USA)

September 21–28
Transamerican Open
San Francisco, USA

1) bt B. Manson (USA) 6–0 6–1
2) bt B. Drewett (Aust) 6–0 6–1
3) bt T. Moor (USA) 6–3 6–2
QF) lost to W. Scanlon (USA) 6–3 6–7 2–6

Won doubles with P. Fleming (USA)

October 7–11
Mazda Challenge Cup
Melbourne, Australia

RR) lost to J. Kriek (SA) 3–6 6–3 6–3
    bt R. Tanner (USA) 6–4 6–4
    bt P. McNamara (Aust) 6–4 6–2
SF) lost to E. Teltscher (USA) 7–6 1–6 3–6

October 12–18
Custom Credit Australian Indoor
Sydney, Australia

1) bt B. Drewett (Aust) 6–1 6–4
2) bt R. Frawley (Aust) 6–1 7–5
QF) bt Tom Gullikson (USA) 6–0 6–1

SF) bt E. Teltscher (USA) 7–5 7–6
 F) bt R. Tanner (USA) 6–4 7–5 6–2

Won doubles with Peter Fleming (USA)

October 26–November 1
Seiko Classic
Tokyo, Japan
 1) bt J. Sadri (USA) 6–2 6–2
 2) bt T. Fukui (Jap) 6–3 6–2
QF) bt W. Scanlon (USA) 6–4 6–3
SF) lost to V. Van Patten (USA) 3–6 5–7

November 9–15
Benson & Hedges Championships
London, England
 1) bt J. Feaver (GB) 6–1 6–1
 2) bt S. Birner (Czech) 6–2 6–2
QF) bt B. Gottfried (USA) 6–1 6–2
SF) bt A. Mayer (USA) 6–3 6–3
 F) lost to J. Connors (USA) 6–3 6–2 3–6 4–6 2–6

November 26–29
Brooklyn Masters
Milan, Italy
RR) bt T. Smid (Czech) 6–0 6–1
     bt A. Panatta (Italy) 6–4 6–2
     bt G. Vilas (Arg) 6–2 6–2
 F) lost to I. Lendl (Czech) 4–6 6–2 4–6

November 30–December 2
America v Europe
Barcelona, Spain
 1) bt Y. Noah (Fr) 6–2 6–7 6–2
 2) bt A. Panatta (Italy) 6–4 6–4
bt I. Lendl (Czech) 4–6 7–6 6–1

Davis Cup Record
1978–1981

1978

September 15–17
v Chile at Santiago, Chile

with B. Gottfried bt B. Prajoux and J. Fillol 3–6 6–3 8–6
6–3

December 8–10
v Great Britain at Palm Springs, USA

bt J. Lloyd 6–1 6–2 6–2
bt C. Mottram 6–2 6–2 6–1

1979

March 16–18
v Colombia at Cleveland, USA

bt A. Betancur 6–2 6–1 6–1
bt I. Molina 6–4 6–3 6–2

with P. Fleming bt I. Molina and O. Agudelo 6–4 6–0
6–4

September 14–16
v Argentina at Memphis, USA

bt G. Vilas 6–2 6–3 6–2
bt J. L. Clerc 6–2 6–3

October 6–8
v Australia at Sydney, Australia

bt J. Alexander 9–7 6–2 9–7
bt M. Edmondson 6–3 6–4

December 14–16
v Italy at San Francisco, USA

bt A. Panatta 6–2 6–3 6–4
bt A. Zugarelli 6–4 6–3 6–1

1980

February 22–24
v Mexico at Mexico City, Mexico

bt R. Ramirez 6–4 6–4 6–3

with P. Fleming bt R. Ramirez and M. Lara 6–3 6–3
10–12 4–6 6–2

March 7–9
v Argentina at Buenos Aires, Argentina

lost to J. L. Clerc 3–6 2–6 6–4 11–13
lost to G. Vilas 2–6 6–4 3–6 6–2 4–6

with P. Fleming bt C. Gattiker and R. Cano 6–0 6–1 6–4

1981

March 6–8
v Mexico at Carlsbad, USA

bt J. Lozano 6–3 6–1 6–3
bt R. Ramirez 6–4 6–3 6–0

July 10–12
v Czechoslovakia at New York, USA

lost to I. Lendl 4–6 12–14 5–7
bt T. Smid 6–3 6–1 6–4

October 2–4
v Australia at Portland, USA

bt M. Edmondson 6–3 6–4 6–2
bt P. McNamara 9–7 6–0

with P. Fleming bt P. McNamara and P. Dent 8–6 6–4
8–6

1981

December 11–13
v Argentina at Cincinnati, USA

bt G. Vilas 6–3 6–2 6–2
bt J. L. Clerc 7–5 5–7 6–3 3–6 6–1

with P. Fleming bt J. L. Clerc and G. Vilas 6–3 4–6 6–4
4–6 11–9

Overall record

Singles – won 18, lost 3
Doubles – won 6, lost 0

Other Arrow Books of interest:

SPORTING FEVER

Michael Parkinson

Ever known a centre-half who could break coconuts with his head? Or a bowler that got bitten by his own false teeth?

Sporting fever runs in the blood. Michael Parkinson inherited the disease from a cricket-crazy grandfather who thought nothing of trudging thirty miles to see Yorkshire play, and it now looks as if his own children have fallen prey to it.

Bill Shankley, Gary Sobers and Muhammed Ali number among the sporting personalities Parkinson has watched, met or played against. But so do some other, less likely characters. . . .

'Parkinson is superb' *Observer*

£1·25

STAND BY YOUR MAN
Tammy Wynette with Joan Dew

From a tarpaper shack in rural Mississippi, to the stage of the Grand Ole Opry in Nashville, this is the movingly personal and honest rags-to-riches story of the Queen of Country Music – Tammy Wynette.

As a child she seemed to spend most of her time down on all fours, fingers cut and knees sore, dusty, dirty and exhausted. As a young wife and mother, beset by problems and unhappiness, struggling just to survive, there seemed little room for dreams. But she always believed that there *had* to be more to life than picking cotton and doing housework. Through poverty and frustration, through hardships and disappointments, Tammy Wynette held tight to her dreams – and to her belief in the power of love.

This is her candid, inspiring story . . .

£1.75

FINCHY
My Life with Peter Finch

Yolande Finch

One of the most personal biographies you will ever read.
She was his lover, his mistress, his wife and his friend. She
was with him as he struggled to the top – and watched help-
lessly as the man she loved began to crumble, threatening to
destroy himself, and her with him.

Now Yolande tells it all – Peter Finch's tragic childhood, his
traumatic affair with Vivien Leigh, his drinking, his women,
his dreams and his failures, his triumphs and heartbreaks . . .
all of it is here. And written as only the woman who really
loved him could tell it.

£1·50

BESTSELLERS FROM ARROW

All these books are available from your bookshop or newsagent or you can order them direct. Just tick the titles you want and complete the form below.

A CHOICE OF CATASTROPHIES	Isaac Asimov	£1.95
BRUACH BLEND	Lillian Beckwith	95p
THE HISTORY MAN	Malcolm Bradbury	£1.60
A LITTLE ZIT ON THE SIDE	Jasper Carrott	£1.25
EENY MEENY MINEY MOLE	Marcel A'Agneau	£1.50
HERO	Leslie Deane	£1.75
TRAVELS WITH FORTUNE	Christine Dodwell	£1.50
11th ARROW BOOK OF CROSSWORDS	Frank Henchard	95p
THE LOW CALORIE MENU BOOK	Joyce Hughes	90p
THE PALMISTRY OF LOVE	David Brandon-Jones	£1.50
DEATH DREAMS	William Katz	£1.25
PASSAGE TO MUTINY	Alexander Kent	£1.50
HEARTSOUNDS	Marth Weinman Lear	£1.75
LOOSELY ENGAGED	Christopher Matthew	£1.25
HARLOT	Margaret Pemberton	£1.60
TALES FROM A LONG ROOM	Peter Tinniswood	£1.50
INCIDENT ON ATH	E. C. Tubb	£1.15
THE SECOND LADY	Irving Wallace	£1.75
STAND BY YOUR MAN	Tammy Wynette	£1.75
DEATH ON ACCOUNT	Margaret Yorke	£1.00
	Postage	
	Total	

ARROW BOOKS, BOOKSERVICE BY POST, PO BOX 29, DOUGLAS, ISLE OF MAN, BRITISH ISLES

Please enclose a cheque or postal order made out to Arrow Books Limited for the amount due including 10p per book for postage and packing for orders within the UK and 12p for overseas orders.

Please print clearly

NAME ....

ADDRESS..

....

Whilst every effort is made to keep prices down and to keep popular books in print, Arrow Books cannot guarantee that prices will be the same as those advertised here or that the books will be available.